the
bargaiN
hunter's
handbook

Andrew Adamides

kandour Ltd

Published by
Kandour Ltd
1-3 Colebrooke Place
London N1 8HZ
United Kingdom

This edition printed in 2005 for
Bookmart Ltd
Registered Number 2372865
Trading As Bookmart Ltd
Blaby Road
Wigston
Leicester LE18 4SE

First published March 2005

Created for Kandour Ltd by Metro Media Ltd
Author: Andrew Adamides
Cover and text design: Paul Barton
Page layout: Sally Stray
Managing editor: Jenny Ross
Photography: photos.com
With thanks to Lee Coventry

© Kandour Ltd

Printed and bound in United Kingdom

ISBN 1-904756-37-9

CONTENTS

Introduction 5

Where to get a bargain 6

How to find a bargain 50

Selling on at a profit 106

Future collectibles 128

Useful web links 140

A–Z Jargon buster 142

CONTENTS

We all like a bargain, as many as possible in fact, particularly as prices seem to escalate on a daily basis. Finding a bargain is often down to luck, although many people just have the knack for searching them out. But knowing the tricks of the trade and applying them to your purchases is by far the most successful way of hunting down an entire range of bargains.

The Bargain Hunter's Handbook will give you the upper hand, detailing the places where you can find the greatest bargains and offering tips on how to make the best of high street sales, auction houses, factory outlets, second-hand shops, online retailers and other resources where bargains are ripe for the picking.

The Bargain Hunter's Handbook also provides a step-by-step guide to the rich diversity of items – from property, financial products and cars to food, clothing, antiques and collectibles – which can be obtained with great savings.

There are also tips on how to sell, with a breakdown of the numerous popular items you may want to offload and advice on how to spot goods which will increase in value over the years.

The A–Z glossary acts as a jargon busting list of terms used by auctioneers, eBayers and other specialists, just to help you talk the talk as well as walking the walk, and the directory of weblinks with help you surf bargains from imported cars to online shopping auctions.

The bargain hunter's most useful weapon is common sense. Cultivate it and you will instinctively know when something is cheaper than it ought to be, when it is over-priced or fake, valuable or worthless. Common sense can help you decide when a potential bargain is just too good to be true and should also prompt to walk away from a deal when you stand a chance of overspending.

The Bargain Hunter's Handbook will help you develop your innate common sense. While some factors in successful bargain hunting are obvious – arriving early at sales and relying on expert information when considering an expensive purchase – it is only when you combine good sense with strong insider knowledge that you will be able to slash your shopping costs and save yourselves considerable amounts of money.

INTRODUCTION

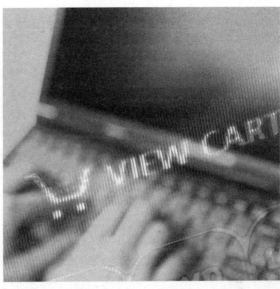

WHERE TO GET A BARGAIN

A uctions have been a popular way to buy and sell for thousands of years. The word 'auction' is derived from the Latin auctio meaning 'to gradually increase', and the earliest recorded auction took place around 500 BC, when the Greek historian Herodotus wrote of women being sold at auction to the highest bidders. The first auctions as we know them today were mentioned in the 1595 Oxford English Dictionary, and the huge houses of Sotheby's and Christie's – the world's most famous auctioneers – were founded in 1744 and 1766 respectively.

At a typical modern auction, items are sold by lot number and go to the highest bidder. If your bid is the highest, you have entered into a legal, binding agreement to buy the goods. Most auction houses require bidders to register at the start of an auction and an agreement to this effect must be signed at that time.

Online auctions aside (these are dealt with later in this book), there are two basic forms:

SEALED BID AUCTION

This is where bidders write down the maximum amount they are willing to pay for the item and seal the bid in an envelope. The vendor then opens these and the highest bid wins. Also known as 'silent auctions', these are usually held for high-value items such as property or at high-profile occasions such as charity events.

OPEN OUTCRY BIDDING

The more widely used and better known version, where bidders call out or otherwise indicate the amount they are willing to pay to the auctioneer.

On registration, some auctioneers supply bidders with a small 'paddle' or sign with an allocated number and direct this to be raised to indicate that a bid is being made. Some specialist auction houses also allow telephone bidding, or absentee bidding, where an offer is submitted in a sealed envelope as per a sealed bid auction.

Generally speaking, tales of auction attendees sneezing or blinking and then finding this has been taken as a sign that they are bidding are just that: tales.

Two commonly applied auction terms are:

DUTCH AUCTION

If a vendor has more than one identical item to sell, they may offer these at a Dutch auction, where the opening bid is the selling price. This is the case unless there are more bidders than there are items, and one or more bidders are willing to pay more than the start price.

So, for example, assume a vendor has 10 television sets and offers these in a Dutch auction with a starting bid of £150 each. If 10 bidders each indicate that they are willing to pay £150 for each TV set, then all the sets will be sold. One will go to each bidder, for the starting bid of £150.

If just nine bidders indicate that they are willing to pay the start price, then each will buy a set at £150, and the tenth TV will remain unsold.

If, however, 10 people indicate that they are willing to pay £150 each for a TV, but an 11th person indicates

that they are willing to pay £175, then the nine bidders who bid first will each get a TV set for £150. The person who bid 10th will be outbid, and the 11th bidder buys the remaining set for £175.

RESERVE PRICE AUCTION

A reserve price is that which must be achieved for an item to be sold. For example, bidding may start on an item at £5, but the reserve may be £100. If the highest bid is just £95, the bidder will not have won the item, as their bid is less than the reserve.

WHAT IS SOLD AT AUCTION?

Generally speaking pretty much anything and everything is auctionable, but the most popular items are grouped under the following headings.

Antiques, Art & Collectibles

This includes furniture, jewellery, artefacts, old toys, clocks, paintings, sculpture, stamps, books, coins and militaria.

Property

Houses, flats, land, offices, shops, factory units and warehouses.

Vehicles

Cars, trucks, buses, caravans, boats and aeroplanes.

Household goods

Furniture, fridges, freezers, washing machines, televisions, beds, carpets and other electrical goods.

Consumable goods

Food and drink.

Office equipment

This includes desks, chairs and filing cabinets.

Computer equipment

Computers, printers and scanners.

Industrial machinery

Printing works, chemical equipment, catering equipment and scrap metal.

Agricultural goods

Buildings, tractors, tools and livestock.

WHY ARE ITEMS SOLD AT AUCTION?

Goods come up for auction for many reasons, and it's extremely important to know why a particular piece is up for sale. It may be because it is surplus to requirements, or because it is defective and the owner wants to sell with no chance of any comeback. The reasons for items being offered at auction do also differ greatly depending on the goods themselves.

1 Goods sold by creditors to recoup money owed by debtors

When individuals or companies become bankrupt, their assets may be seized and are sometimes disposed of via auction. Often in these cases the items are in excellent working order.

2 Goods offered by dealers who want to make a profit

In many cases, dealers will buy items cheaply and then offer them at auction with the hope of selling at a higher price. This is common with antiques and classic cars. The dealer knows an auction will be attended by many potential buyers and so there is the opportunity to make a higher profit than if the item were sold in a shop and to do so quickly.

WHERE TO GET A BARGAIN

3   Items sold to make space for new stock

Often, surplus goods, which are out-dated, may be offered at auction in order for retailers to restock their shelves and warehouses. While these may be obsolete, there is also scope for picking up bargains if up-to-the-minute specifications are not required, such as, when buying a computer.

4   Items have been over-ordered and are surplus to requirements

Again, there is the potential of a bargain here, with over-ordered new items often selling for prices way below retail value.

5   Items have been leased out and the lease has expired

People and companies often choose to lease rather than buy vehicles, furniture or computer equipment, paying only for the depreciation in value, so that they can update their equipment easily. Returned products can be sold off cheaply.

6 Goods in over-supply which cannot be disposed of any other way

Here is an opportunity to pick up items extremely cheaply, although bear in mind, that if you intend to sell on you will need to be sure that there will be a demand.

7 Items confiscated by the authorities

Another potential source of bargains, though be aware that items confiscated by the police, customs or other government departments may have been in storage for a long time and may have deteriorated as a result. Also, if seized under certain conditions, the goods may also have suffered damage as a result of this.

8 Goods may have been stolen and are being auctioned by insurers

Often, stolen goods are written off by insurers and are then sold to recoup some of the money paid out to their former owners. These items will usually be damaged, but for those seeking, for example, cars to dismantle for parts, auctions like these can be a goldmine. Very often insurers write-off older vehicles or equipment which may only be slightly damaged, although this is an area where specialist knowledge is a must.

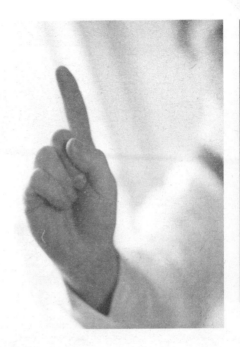

9 Government surplus

This sort of auction can produce all manner of goods, from clothing to office equipment to foodstuffs, but do bear in mind that, again, such items may be either out-of-date or have been in storage for long periods of time, which may render them obsolete or have resulted in a deterioration in their condition.

OBTAINING A BARGAIN AT AUCTION

Never rush headlong into buying at auction. First be aware of the hidden costs. Most auctioneers charge a 10% fee on top of the final hammer (sale)

WHERE TO GET A BARGAIN

price and there is VAT to pay at 17.5%. Paying by credit card may result in a further extra charge, usually 3%, to cover processing. Altogether, these fees can add 30% to the original sale price.

It is important that you know your market. Attend several auctions for similar items to whatever you want to buy and see how much items go for. This will give you a firmer understanding of how much you should be prepared to bid. Also, don't be carried away by the spirit of competition. That's one reason for

auctions: vendors hope buyers will become locked into a bidding war and increase the price. Always be wary; unscrupulous auctioneers are known to plant fake bidders in the crowd to drive up the prices. Usually there is no way of knowing who these people are, but bear this in mind when tempted to go just that little bit higher.

When it comes to art and antiques, specialist auctioneers know how much items should sell for. These auctions are usually attended by bidders who have a similar appreciation for the value of individual items. Since it is highly unlikely you will turn up a bargain at Sotheby's, seek out auctioneers who specialise in estate sales, or smaller auction houses where the goal is to get rid of items rather than obtain the highest price. Bear in mind when buying a set of items together that you may be able to offset the cost of acquiring one particular item by reselling the other, unwanted goods which come along with it.

Always read the small print in the catalogue and remember that buyers' rights are different for items bought at auction. Unless the description in the catalogue explicitly states that an item is fully functioning, you will not be able to get your money back if you discover it doesn't work. There is an exception: if it causes personal injury or more than £275 worth of damage to your property there is recourse for compensation. Often, auctioneers can

be wily. Instead of stating condition by the item name, they may use footnotes, grading an item by number where 1 is denoted in the small print as 'slight damage', 2 as 'badly worn' and 3 as 'not functioning'. Always read the small print on the agreement you sign when registering as a bidder, as this will state the terms of sale. These may include such stipulations as you having to remove whatever you buy from the auctioneer's premises on the day of the auction. If you don't, you may end up having to pay extortionate storage fees. It is also quite common that payment is acceptable only by cash or cheque.

FINDING AUCTIONS

Auction houses are listed in telephone directories, where there will also be adverts detailing what sort of items they specialise in. Many operate websites and a telephone call or online visit should reveal all you need to know about attending one of their auctions. Specialist auction houses selling antiques and classic cars advertise widely in publications geared towards those interested in purchasing such items, so reading these magazines should yield plenty of background information. For government auctions of seized property and surplus stock the best thing to do is to surf the net, use

your search engine to find 'UK government auctions' in your locale. This should turn up contact information and dates of events and you will also be able to join a mailing list to receive regular updates on what's coming up for auction and when.

Property and (non-classic, non-exotic) car auctions are often the most difficult to gain information about, but they are also the most likely places to turn up bargains. There is a reason for

this. For a considerable time, these were only open to traders and indeed some still are. Generally speaking, property auctions are still fairly hard to get into. There are several professional services you can use to send you information, but at a price. If you see a 'For sale by auction' sign outside a property, take a note of the company's name and ask to be put on the their mailing list.

Car auctions are a little easier to

access, largely thanks to the internet, by entering 'UK car auctions' into your search engine. Again, there are numerous professionals prepared to buy on your behalf at auction, usually for a fee. Their insider knowledge may prove invaluable. Knowledge of these events also tends to spread by word of mouth.

AUCTIONS CHECKLIST
1. Know all the costs involved
2. Know your market
3. Don't get carried away by competition
4. Aim for smaller auction houses
5. Read the small print

GENERAL TERMS OF SALE
Following are examples of the terms of sale you may find at an auction.

1 Merchandise must be as described in the catalogue, but no warranty is implied unless explicitly stated.

2 All potential buyers must register in advance of the auction.

3 Purchases must be removed from the auctioneer's premises at the buyer's expense after payment is made in full on the day of the auction.

4 Bids may be submitted by an agent acting on behalf of a bidder if the bidder cannot attend the auction.

5 All winning bids will be subject to a premium of 10% with VAT at 17.5% and payments by credit card to a further charge of 3% of the total.

Note: These terms may vary with every auction so always check in advance.

BOOT FAIRS & JUMBLE SALES

Generally speaking, jumble sales tend to be held by churches, schools or local organisations as a way of raising money by selling off donated items. They are usually fairly small in size.

Car boot sales (or boot fairs), on the other hand, range in size from a few cars to huge fields of vehicles, which can take an entire day to walk around. The money raised goes to the individual sellers. There will also be semi-professional traders who specialise in goods such as music, DVDs or antiques.

WHAT ARE THE BARGAINS?

Basically, anything sells at these events and bargains can come in many forms – just be prepared to look for them. All but the most chaotic jumble sales separate out clothes from toys, books, household items and ornaments. Many jumble sale organisers issue limits on what they are looking for when asking for donations, accepting only clothes, household items or books.

A visit to a car boot sale, however, can turn up pretty much anything and everything and the quality is often better than at jumble sales. The fact

WHERE TO GET A BARGAIN

that there is direct personal gain involved means that vendors are prepared to present goods in acceptable condition.

As there are no category limits with car boot sales, people sell almost anything. For the most part though, items also tend to be small, since they will have been transported in a car.

The following items are often found at both boot fairs and jumble sales:

Clothes
Books
Toys
Small ornaments/collectibles
Videos/DVDs

Car boot sales are also a source of:
Furniture
Electrical goods
Larger ornamental/household /collectible items

BOOT FAIRS AND JUMBLE SALES CHECKLIST

1. Go for events in affluent areas
2. Get there early
3. Look around thoroughly
4. Be prepared to haggle
5. Don't let on if you find a bargain
6. Dress comfortably
7. Don't take risks with potentially dangerous purchases

HUNTING DOWN A BARGAIN

Now for the tricky bit. As there is usually an awful lot of rubbish at both types of event, finding a bargain requires resourcefulness.

1 Pick a jumble/car boot sale in a wealthy area

Events held in wealthier neighbourhoods are more likely to offer good-quality, newer or more expensive items, increasing the likelihood of finding a bargain. There is also a better chance of finding antique/collectible objects, since larger properties and higher incomes can result in a higher turnover of items.

2 Arrive as early as possible

At boot sales, this is around 7 am to catch the vendors arriving before the event starts. They may well have had time to go through what everyone else is offering and pick out the best bargains for themselves, so if you are selling at a boot sale, make sure to take a friend or partner. They can set up while you have a look round at what everyone else has got. Even if they refuse to sell before the fair officially opens (which most won't), you'll know who has what and can nip back to buy as soon as doors open.

3 Rummage thoroughly

Often there are large boxes full of items, so what you want could be buried at the bottom. Make sure you take a good look around, especially if there are similar items to whatever you want on the table.

4 Be prepared to haggle at car boot sales

Prices tend to be slightly higher than they are at jumble sales, but vendors do not want to take anything home with them, so will often come down a bit in order to obtain a sale. This is especially the case when nearing closing time, although leaving it that late in the day may be risky since the bargains are usually snapped up first thing. Haggling at jumble sales is not usually done, since the proceeds are going to charity.

5 Don't let on if someone's just sold you a bargain

Remain calm at all times. If the vendor hasn't handed over the item and recognises the fact that they have under priced, they are quite within

their rights to renegotiate.

6 Dress comfortably and dress down

For one thing, you may be walking a long way if it's a large boot sale and you want to be as comfy as possible. For another, if you are clad head-to-toe in designer gear, it's unlikely that a vendor will agree to come down on a price because they'll think you can afford more.

7 Be aware of the risks of purchase

Buying at car boot and jumble sales doesn't come with cast iron guarantees of quality. Check that anything with multiple pieces is complete and be aware that there is a possibility that electrical items may not work. Since most of the vendors will be private obtaining a refund will be highly unlikely. Boot sales are hard to police and as such can attract rogue traders. DVDs, CDs and games may be pirated, while toys may not conform to safety regulations. Neither may soft furnishings or electrical goods. Boot vendors are classed as traders only if:
• they sell items bought expressly for that purpose, rather than selling their own property
• they sell on a regular basis
• they employ people to help them.

WHERE TO GET A BARGAIN

There is greater legal recourse for protection with traders, as they must display a business name and address, must not sell anything unsafe or display signs limiting buyers' rights, eg. 'No Refunds'. However, bear in mind that suing someone can be a laborious process and if the trader doesn't have the cash to cough up (as many cowboy traders won't), it can be fruitless. Better to buy wisely and find that bargain than have to deal with the aftermath of a bad buy.

FINDING JUMBLE AND CAR BOOT SALES

Jumble sales are usually advertised on church, school or town hall notice boards, or via flyers handed out locally. Always check locations where ads are placed for free: outside community centres, local surgeries and civic halls.

Car boot sales are advertised in similar ways, but are also detailed in numerous calendars and on several websites such as www.carbootcalendar.com and www.carbootjunction.com. Small subscription fees may apply. Internet search engines are a rich source of information. Type in 'car boot sale' and the name of the locale you are searching for, and you will doubtless turn up plenty of information.

MARKETS, FLEA MARKETS & COLLECTORS' FAIRS

The definitions of markets, flea markets and collector's fairs differs from country to country and region to region around the world.

Items typically on sale at UK markets include:

Clothes
Bags & Luggage
Toys
Ornaments
Stationery
Toiletries
DVDs, Videos & CDs
Books
Food (fresh or packaged)
Plants and flowers

Some markets house stalls selling antiques or collectibles, but as the cost of stall rental increases, these appear more often in specialist markets and collectors' fairs. Other markets specialise in fresh food (often referred to as farmers' markets) or clothes, books or flowers.

Flea market is a term more commonly used in the US and Europe. In the UK, they are more likely to be referred to as antique markets. Generally, flea markets have an emphasis on antiques and collectibles. Items at flea markets tend to command higher prices as many stall-holders are also dealers who know the value of items on display. The term flea market originally comes from the French name

Marche aux Puces, given to a market in Paris which sold second-hand and more than likely flea-infested clothes to the poor.

Flea markets are usually more extensive than ordinary markets, and many of the most famous ones in Europe – such as the regular one in Lille in northern France – can also be pricey as they cater to tourists.

Items commonly for sale at flea markets include:

Lamps, light fittings and mirrors
Toys, statuettes, vases and stamps
Miscellaneous unusual items like shop mannequin's, antique medical or sports equipment

Books
Vintage clothing
Jewellery

Collectors' fairs also known as swap meets tend to be organised at a public venue such as a school hall and take place every month or so, catering specifically to collectors of one type of product, usually antiques, such as toys or model trains. The name is derived from the practice of collectors bringing in unwanted goods and 'swapping' them with stall-holders for items they desire. This practice still continues, with many stall-holders happy to enact exchanges.

WHAT BARGAINS ARE THERE?

Ordinary markets are a source of bargains but the quality of toys, clothes, fragrances and household products may be low. However, certain goods, such as luggage, can be better value than in retail outlet shops.

Best buys from markets include:

Fresh produce – ensure you buy from a reputable vendor. Prices are usually lower than those paid in supermarkets.

Stationery – tape, wrapping paper, scissors, rulers, pens and pencils can all be bought at knock-down prices, far cheaper than in high street stationery shops.

Books – both paperbacks and hardbacks are available. Many book vendors operate a "buy-back" policy on paperbacks. This means that you can buy, read, then sell back at a reduced rate.

DVDs/Videos/CDs – Many vendors operate a buy-back scheme or have used sections for DVDs and CDs. This can often represent a considerable saving on shop prices, although it is important to beware of traders selling pirated items.

Flea markets and collectors' fairs can be sources of bargains, but it depends on what you are looking for. As most of the traders have a good idea of what their items are worth on the open market, bargains are harder to find. The exceptions occur when looking for an item that is particularly rare. This may

WHERE TO GET A BARGAIN

not be in demand with collectors, and consequently will be sold cheap due to lack of demand. Also, these events can be good for spare parts for restoration of damaged collectibles or furniture.

WHY ARE ITEMS SOLD AT THESE MARKETS?

Markets provide a cheap means of making sales without the overheads of running a shop. Many of the items are 'seconds' sold on by shops or distributors, often at auction. Other goods are second-hand or have been bought directly from producers or wholesalers.

The high cost of renting some market stalls means that some traders choose to sell their goods at car boot sales, where pitches tend to be cheaper.

Similarly, flea markets provide a way for dealers to sell antiques and vintage items, which may not be offered by antique shops or specialist auctioneers, for example, due to their being damaged.

HUNTING DOWN A BARGAIN AT A MARKET, FLEA MARKET OR COLLECTORS' FAIR

At ordinary markets, there's sometimes a little room for haggling on items with high price tags, and often, stall holders will reduce the price if you buy in large quantities.

There may also be fresh produce bargains on whatever is left over at the end of the day. Do remember, however, that there may be a reason why it is left over. Book or DVD vendors often provide two-for-one or three-for-two price special offers, which will usually be boldly advertised.

At flea markets and collectors' fairs always:

1 Carry plenty of cash in small denominations

Vendors may not have change. Cheques will usually be accepted but few vendors will accept credit or debit cards. It's also harder to haggle if you are paying by Amex, rather than if you are offering a few crumpled up notes as all the money you have on you.

2 Haggle

And be prepared to do so far more sternly than if buying at a boot sale, because price tags will be higher.

Know your market, know the market value and don't rush into purchases you know are over-priced unless the item is rare.

3 Be prepared to walk away

Just as at an auction, if you can't get an item for what you want to pay, you know you don't want to spend more and you know it's not worth more, you should walk away. This may even spur the vendor into calling you back and offering a further price reduction.

4 Wear comfortable clothes and make sure your apparel has big pockets

You'll be doing a lot of walking at most

large flea markets and the majority of the items will be small, so you'll want to be able to carry them easily. Make sure you take a bag and some protective wrap, as some vendors may not provide this and you'll want your new treasures to be well-protected. And again, don't forget to dress down. You really won't get dealers selling you things at cut-price rates if it's clear you can afford to pay more.

5 **Arrive early**
Bargains go fast and everybody wants one. You'll be annoyed if you show up long after opening time and see someone else walking off with exactly what you were looking for and you'll never know how much they paid for it, either.

6 **Take a small screwdriver or Swiss army knife and tape measure** This will help you measure and dismantle larger items for easier carrying.

7 **Plan your route**
If it is a large flea market like those in Paris, take a map and plan your route to make sure you see everything you want. Flea markets are often not the most organised of places, and you don't want to miss a bargain because you didn't happen to walk down one particular alley.

FINDING MARKETS, FLEA MARKETS AND COLLECTORS' FAIRS
Often larger more out-of-the-way markets advertise with flyers or posters, generally in places where it's free to advertise, so check all the places you'd look for car boot or jumble sale ads, like church notice boards, community centre ad posting boards or supermarket posting boards. Any large market will attract a lot of buyers, so ask around. As always, internet searches are helpful, too.

Well-established or large markets tend to be fairly well-known and are often featured in city guides. They are less likely to advertise. Antiques markets which aren't permanent will

MARKETS, SWAP MEETS AND FLEA MARKETS CHECKLIST

1. Carry lots of change and smaller denomination notes

2. Be prepared to haggle

3. Be prepared to walk away from a sale

4. Dress comfortably

5. Get there early

6. Don't forget your tools

7. Plot your route

often advertise with posters, or in specialist or local press. UK collectors' fairs are almost exclusively advertised in the specialist press by their promoters. Check ads in specialist magazines covering collectibles for telephone numbers and e-mail addresses.

In all cases, don't forget to check opening days and times and whether they are seasonal, as some close for part of the year.

ONLINE SHOPPING

The internet has revolutionised consumer society and not only the way we shop but also the way we hunt for bargains. According to research, the number of people shopping online doubles approximately every six months and about two-thirds of all the purchases made are for less than £50.

Online shops are split into two categories: the online catalogue versions of high-street and other physical retailers and those cybertraders who sell exclusively via the net. Some of the former do not allow online purchasing. Instead you may browse their products and buy in stores. Others will let you make purchases from the comfort of your computer, although they may operate internet-only offers, where you can download coupons and take these into shops in order to obtain discounts.

Buying from an online shop should be as simple a sales transaction as possible. Use the search engine to find the product you are interested in, view the photographs and read the specifications, then follow the instructions, usually either clicking on a product or using a tick box to mark it and add it to your online shopping cart. You then proceed to the checkout, where postage or delivery charges (if applicable) will be added. Details of

how to contact the company (usually by telephone or e-mail) and their returns policy are available on all reputable websites.

The second means of net shopping, and potentially the most revolutionary, is via auction. Internet auctions were pioneered by the company eBay, whose name has become indelibly associated with this activity. eBay was launched in 1995 by a businessman named Pierre Omidyar, who invented the online auction format in order that his wife, a collector of Pez sweet dispensers, could trade with other fans.

eBay has been likened to a global flea market/car boot sale/collectors' fair. On an average day over 19 million items are listed for sale in 35,000 categories and

many of these are potential bargains.

Most online auctions are simple to understand and use. You register, choose a username and password, and then bid on items found by entering keywords into the site's search engine, or through browsing the listings. Each individual auction has a deadline and the highest bid at the end, winds. Buyers can bid as many times as they like. Like real-world auctioneers, most online sites offer a reserve price and Dutch auctions.

eBay is by far the largest auctioneer on the net, though competitors cater for a particular niche market. Some specialise in certain areas – computers, for example – and work in more of a 'sealed-bid' manner, whereby they detail lots available and invite bids to be submitted. Some of these sites charge VAT and a premium on top of the final hammer price, much like a traditional auctioneer.

In addition to these types of online shopping, there are also online classified sections, which function in a similar manner to newspaper ads, in that people can simply advertise items for sale.

WHAT ARE THE ONLINE BARGAINS?

If you are prepared to spend time surfing you should be able to turn up bargains in almost any sphere. Auctions are a fantastic source of bargains on antiques and collectibles. Online retailers, meanwhile, offer bargains on all the following:

Electrical goods

Books

CDs

DVDs

Holidays and air tickets

Financial products, from credit cards to mortgages

Concert & event tickets

Food can also be bought online, thanks to the advent of online supermarkets, but most usually charge a one-off delivery fee to cover transportation costs.

WHY ARE ITEMS SOLD ONLINE?

Selling online has numerous advantages. To online-only retailers, it allows them to reduce overheads and pass the savings on to their customers, giving lower prices and higher sales figures.

To 'real-world' shops, it provides added sales as customers can browse and shop from the comfort of their own home, rather than going out to the shop itself. That way, they can target those who either don't know where the nearest branch is, or who don't have time to go there, but who can easily log onto the website for a few minutes to make their purchase.

For auctioneers, it provides a global audience for their merchandise, meaning that they aren't just limited to selling to whoever attends a 'real' auction and the bidders who call in on the phone. With a global marketplace, more collectors and interested parties can view the items on sale, and higher

prices can often be realised, especially as some items can be far more collectible in some parts of the world than they are in others.

HUNTING DOWN AN ONLINE BARGAIN

Always use this checklist:

1 **Check that the vendor is reputable**

If buying from one of the smaller, less well-known online retailers, ensure that there is a customer service telephone number (which works) displayed on the website and an address where the company is registered, which should not be a PO Box number.

2 **Check as wide a range of prices as possible**

The internet is filled to the brim with retailers selling similar goods, and prices vary hugely. Check out several websites to find your product at the lowest price comparisons. They allow you to enter the name of the product you want and they will compare prices on other online retailers.

Do be aware, however, that you will be buying from a retailer and not from the comparison agent itself and, as such, you need to ensure that the retailer is reputable. Also, bear in mind that some comparison agents may be in partnership with the retailers, and will turn these results up as 'featured listings' or similar, marked out in bold, or in front of the other prices listed, when they might not be the cheapest. Always read the search results in full before buying.

Comparison agents work for a wide variety of items, from DVDs to computers to washing machines, and there are similar agents who are useful to compare holiday or airline ticket prices. However, when buying items such as theatre or concert tickets, it is not usual to use a comparison agent. In these cases always make sure to check with the venue before buying from a ticket agency to ensure it really has sold out if that is claimed and that prices are not being artificially inflated.

3 Online-only specials

Numerous shops with 'real-world' presence use their websites to sell refurbished items and seconds along with new stock in their shops. This is often the case with electrical retailers, and many of these goods come with identical warranties to their new counterparts. Sign up for newsletters from your favourite retailer and you should also find special offers being e-mailed to you for both online and offline shops. This is often the case if the vendor does not sell online. Some retailers selling smaller items such as books and CDs allow people to list second-hand copies alongside the new ones too. These can often be a considerable saving on 'new' prices, especially when shopping for items such as student textbooks.

4 Check the shipping costs

Check the cost of delivery and factor it into your purchase. Most comparison agents include the cost of shipping in the results they give for items and many online retailers offer various different shipping options at different prices. Some may even deliver for free, while others offer the option

of collecting an item from one of their shops.

5 Make sure that you are buying securely

When sending sensitive information, always make sure you are buying on a secure server. You can check this by making sure that a small padlock is displayed in the CLOSED position at the bottom of your internet browser, over to the right hand side of the screen. The system should also notify you automatically if there are any problems with the site security and will alert you with a dialogue box when you leave a secure server connection .

6 When shopping online, always use a credit card, PayPal or similar online payment system

These offer you far more protection than sending a cheque or money order, as you have a means of redress if the goods arrive late or not at all.

7 Take extra care when shopping for items that may look different on screen

Internet browsers and creative photography can distort the colours and sizes of clothes, furniture and other items. Any item where size or colour should be taken into consideration should be viewed with great care. Always read the returns policy carefully before the purchase is made.

8 Always take care when buying internationally

While a favourable exchange rate can offer bargains, be aware that when purchasing from sources overseas, returns are very difficult to arrange, shipping costs can be exorbitant and buyer protection – even through credit cards – may be less effective.

Finding bargains through online auctions should be approached in a similar manner as purchasing in the real world: don't bid more than you can afford or want to and don't ignore buyers' premiums if buying through a site which charges them. When buying on auction sites, however, here are some tricks and tips to ensure bargains:

more items, as someone may have listed just what you want as part of a bigger lot, without putting the name in the auction title.

1 Bid as late as possible

Especially in the case of desirable items, bidders usually wait until the last minute. This has two advantages: firstly, it avoids driving the price up early in the auction and also for the simple reason that nobody can outbid you if the auction has ended. Often the price of an item can double in the last 30 seconds of the auction.

2 Search by both the auction title and the auction text

This has the effect of turning up far

3 Search for common misspellings of item names

This is an excellent way to obtain a bargain, as often users don't type names in correctly. If the item cannot be found, it cannot be bid for, which means you will be able to pick it up for a song.

4 Check feedback ratings

Many internet vendors operate a 'feedback' system, allowing buyers and vendors to rate each other on how well the transaction went. There are options

to leave positive, neutral and negative feedback. Clearly a vendor with many negatives should be avoided.

HOW TO FIND ONLINE SHOPPING SITES

Many online shops are now so well known that – like eBay and Amazon – their names have entered popular vernacular. Finding the websites of well-known retailers such as these is relatively easy, be they online-only or online and real-world, as most have simply used their name as the web address with the common suffixes and prefixes: 'www', '.co.uk' or '.com'.

Alternately, well-known shops can be found via search engines and comparison agents can be found in a similar way using keywords like 'compare prices'. Shopping portal sites

SHOPPING ONLINE CHECKLIST

1. Only buy from reputable sellers
2. Compare prices
3. Look for special deals
4. Check shipping costs
5. Only buy on a secure server
6. Use a credit card or online payment system
7. Check the returns policy
8. Take care when buying from abroad

ONLINE AUCTIONS CHECKLIST

1. Bid towards the end of the auction
2. Search title and text
3. Check for misspelling of item names
4. Only buy from sellers with good feedback ratings

or 'online malls' also offer links to many different online shops.

WHERE TO GET A BARGAIN

SALES, OUTLETS, SECOND-HAND & CHARITY SHOPS

Sales are traditionally held in January, and again at the end of summer, when shops need to clear leftover stock and replace it with the new season's merchandise. They do this by reducing the price on whatever they have left of the old stock, and, in the case of the January sales, to boost business in the traditionally slow post-Christmas period. Prices are slashed as the sale period wears on.

Outlet shops, on the other hand, operate low price policies all year, as traditionally they occupied part of the space of the manufacturing plants which produced their goods. Initially they were used to sell-off lines which were either left over from previous seasons or discontinued, or which had minor faults or flaws which precluded selling through the normal shop. While factory outlets still exist, there are now plenty of shops which deal with more than one manufacturer, selling 'seconds' across the board from many makers and carrying a range of items, usually name-branded or designer goals.

Second-hand shops are obviously those which specialise in previously owned items and deal across a broad range of products, from furniture, and bric-a-brac, to clothes (particularly nearly-new designer wear) and household items. All of these will have been bought from previous owners with a view to selling at a profit yet at a price that's cheaper than new.

Charity shops have been around in the UK since 1948, when Oxfam opened their first branch in Broad Street, Oxford. These sell donated items with the money going to the charity they represent. Goods are generally low-priced, meaning the benefits are two-fold: you can find a bargain AND contribute to a good cause.

As with all other potential bargain

sources, there are several ways to approach shopping during the sales or by visiting second-hand and charity shops in order to make sure you maximise your chances of getting a good deal.

As far as the sales go, you should always:

1 Go round shops before the sales start

Note what you want and how much it is, then ask if it will be in the sale, make sure the price has been reduced by an attractive amount before buying.

2 Check stock

If the price hasn't gone down by enough, find out how many of the item they have in stock. If they have plenty and you have the nerve, sit it out. The price is certain to go down towards the end of the sale when the retailer becomes keen to free up space.

3 Go to the right sales

The cheaper the shop, the less likely that super-bargains will be available. Conversely during designers' sales there are a lot of bargains to be had.

4 Show up as early as possible

As with car boot fairs and

practically everything else (except online auctions) you need to get in as early as possible if interested in items you know are likely to sell out quickly.

When shopping at factory outlets and second-hand stores:

1 Check out specialist and regular shops

If you are looking for designer gear, study the shops that specialise in selling it second-hand. You will pay a premium, but they're more likely to have what you want. Alternately, for an antique lamp, go to a place that specialises in large second-hand furniture items; they may have acquired just what you want in a job lot house clearance.

2 Find out delivery days

Know what day deliveries are made, then time your visits to obtain the best pickings.

3 Visit high-income areas

As with boot fairs and jumble sales, charity shops in wealthier areas generally stock better-quality items such as designer label goods.

4 Be prepared to haggle

Not in outlets and charity shops but at second-hand shops you may well be able to barter the price down, especially if you buy more than one item.

DISCOVERING SALES, FACTORY OUTLETS, SECOND-HAND AND CHARITY SHOPS

Sales are usually well publicised in advance, though it's worth noting that while even Harrods makes public its sale, some designer shops do not as a means of retaining exclusivity. In fact some only make sales known and open to valued repeat customers – you could try calling up, pretending to be a client and asking when and where sales are happening.

Outlets and good second-hand shops can be well kept secrets, so ask around, especially for the latter, check the yellow pages for your area or look in city guide books and student publications, which can be a goldmine for information. Bear in mind that plenty of outlets are also online and

can be tracked down by using your search engine.

SALES, OUTLETS, SECOND-HAND AND CHARITY SHOPS CHECKLIST – SALES

1. Know what you want to buy before the sale starts
2. Take a risk and wait for prices to drop further
3. Choose your shops carefully
4. Get there early

CHECKLIST – OUTLETS, SECOND-HAND SHOPS AND CHARITY SHOPS

1. Specialist shops can save you time
2. Know when deliveries are coming in
3. Go to shops in high-income areas
4. Be prepared to haggle

WAREHOUSE SHOPPING CLUBS

Members-only warehouse shopping clubs first occurred in the US and have now spread to the UK and other parts of the world. The idea behind them is simple: members can buy items in bulk at wholesale prices, thereby saving cash in the process. The shops are housed in huge spaces stacked from floor to ceiling with goods. While not run-down, these stores do tend to be spartan and thereby save money on some of the nicer trimmings found in supermarkets. Generally, they have fewer staff and services as a further means of reducing overhead costs and passing them onto the consumer.

Most warehouse shops allow non-members to visit, but in order to buy, you have to be a member. Different chains have different rules, but for the most part membership is limited to:

TRADE MEMBERS

Those who can prove they are the owner or manager of a registered company. Proof requirements vary, but acceptable evidence usually includes a VAT receipt, invoice from another supplier or utility bill.

Some chains limit membership to tradespeople, but others will allow a second category of membership:

PRIVATE INDIVIDUALS

Private membership is usually offered to people who either belong to certain professions, or who have retired from them. Professions included again vary from chain to chain, but most include:

Airline personnel
Accountants
Banking employees
Teachers
Civil Servants
Police personnel
Medical personnel

Legal workers: solicitors and barristers
Architects
Local government workers
Insurance workers

Chains charge annual membership fees from around £12 to £25 plus VAT depending on the particular chain and the membership category being applied for. Most allow members to bring friends in with them (although they may limit the number at any one time). Loaning of membership cards to friends is not permitted. Some require the member's picture to be on the membership card to prevent this from occurring. Opening hours are also unusual, in that some warehouses open only to tradespeople in the morning, with private members granted access in the afternoons and at weekends.

WHAT BARGAINS ARE THERE AT WAREHOUSE SHOPPING CLUBS?

Warehouses offer pretty much everything available at the modern supermarket – and sometimes more. Items on sale include:

Electrical items – fridges, freezers, washing machines and computers.

Generally, there won't be as wide a range as in electrical superstores, but prices will be lower on large goods and all come with guarantees. Warehouses don't usually deliver.

Household items – cleaning equipment, garden equipment, small furniture, household accessories

A wide range of household items will be carried, but don't expect too much range within the item types on offer. Prices should be low, however, especially for high-quality products. Cleaning fluids are available in huge quantities at massive savings.

Clothes – designer, name brand and luxury items.

While again, there may not be a huge choice of ranges, designer brands are stocked at lower-than-usual prices.

Food and drink – fresh and frozen.

The speciality of warehouse clubs. Food, toiletries and alcohol are all much cheaper than in regular retail environments.

idea was to allow them to buy large quantities to sell on at a profit.

FINDING BARGAINS AT WAREHOUSE SHOPPING CLUBS

Remember:

1 Always buy in bulk
The more you buy, the bigger the savings. You may well end up spending far more than you would in a similar supermarket visit, but what you buy will last longer. But you'll need storage space, including in the freezer for perishables.

2 Compare prices with online and retail shops
Not everything is cheaper. Prices for DVDs, CDs and some computer hardware are comparable with high street shops and can on occasion be beaten by online retailers.

3 No delivery
You will have to cover the cost of this yourself since these stores are geared towards tradespeople who tend to own goods vehicles.

4 Watch out for specials
Like ordinary supermarkets, warehouses do make special offers. You will still be buying in bulk, but at even lower prices.

Some warehouses also feature photograph developing outlets, reasonable restaurants, opticians, tyre-fitters and bathroom/kitchen shops.

WHY ARE ITEMS SOLD AT WAREHOUSE SHOPPING CLUBS?

Goods sold at warehouses are generally not seconds, damaged or used. As these warehouses were initially designed for tradespeople only, the

5 VAT
Some items don't carry VAT. For those that do, the tax is added US-style at the counter when you pay and isn't included in the price tag, so don't forget to factor this in to price considerations.

6 Check out affiliates
Some warehouses have affiliations with other retailers who carry items they may not, such as furniture and building suppliers, and members may be entitled to preferential prices at these establishments as well.

7 Take your card with you when you go abroad
Many warehouse chains are international and membership can be used while travelling.

FINDING WAREHOUSE SHOPPING CLUBS

The main chains have their own websites, which can be found in the usual manner, by using a search engine with the keywords 'shopping club warehouse'.

Alternatively, if you fall into one of the membership categories, ask your professional organisation or union for details of the nearest warehouse chain.

CLASSIFIED ADVERTISEMENTS

Classifieds are a cheap form of print or online advertising, placed by individuals buying and sell items. 'Classified' into different categories, these can be found at the back of local, regional, national and trade newspapers and there are also dedicated publications which exclusively feature classified ads, such as *Loot* or *Exchange and Mart*.

Meanwhile specialist publications such as *Classic Car* magazine, solely feature classifieds targeting a particular readership.

BARGAINS AMONG THE CLASSIFIEDS

Items sold in the classified sections range from clothing, stamps and cars, TVs and even holidays. If you're prepared to look hard enough and often enough, you'll probably eventually find bargains on pretty much anything. Scan them regularly, checking in as many places as possible and remember, if you see something you like, act quickly. If the advert is placed in a publication with high circulation, such as Loot, genuine bargains tend to be snapped up.

Since many of the items sold through the classifieds are from private individuals, you are not afforded the same protection as you would when purchasing from a dealer. Take the utmost care to make sure you aren't buying items which may prove problematic, whatever the asking price. Genuine bargains appear relatively rarely so look in smaller circulation publications such as local papers, as these may contain bargains nobody else will see, due to the fact that far fewer people pick up on them.

WHY ARE ITEMS SOLD IN CLASSIFIEDS?

People usually use the classified ads because they provide a venue for selling where the advert will be seen by plenty of potential buyers, without having to involve a professional dealer, or own a shop.

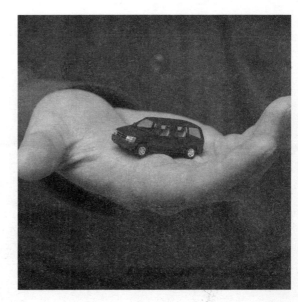

HOW TO FIND A BARGAIN

Buying an antique or collectible at a bargain price is a particular pleasure: it is satisfaction enough to actually find something for which you've been searching for years, but to acquire it at less than market value is especially enjoyable.

As we become increasingly savvy about the value of antiques, bargains become more rare. Not only is it hard to find collectable or antique items at less than the market value, but it is often difficult to find them even at the market value.

Values fluctuate downwards, so it is important to know the current market value of an item and to stick to that when buying.

One aspect of buying smaller collectibles is that they may turn up at almost any of our bargain sources. Larger items such as furniture are a little harder to find as bargains, but that shouldn't stop you from looking.

AUCTIONS

Auction rooms have long been one of the collector's favourite haunts. The fact that auctions are well known as a source of antiques and collectibles does, however, make finding a bargain more difficult. Nevertheless, there are several ways in which to maximise the chances of finding bargains:

1 Seek out smaller auctioneers
See if you can find any that are outside cities or run by small companies. Chances are that fewer people will know about them and as a result there will be fewer attendees. The flip side is, of course, that what they offer may not be of as good quality as the larger houses.

2 Avoid the specialists – but follow the dealers
Seek out estate auctions because these aim to clear houses, not hold out for the highest prices for their items. Bear in mind that if you go where the dealers go, but are buying for yourself, then you still have a good chance of outbidding them. Dealers have to make sure that whatever they buy is purchased at a low enough price for them to make a healthy profit when selling on. Private buyers, however, may generally go a little higher without having to pay the price for the item if bought directly from an antique shop.

Additionally, make sure to look for auctioneers selling items with which they may be unfamiliar. If the auction house usually sells modern furniture, but has suddenly come across a cache of older items, then it may be that they will be unaware of the true value and that other parties interested in buying it will be less likely to attend the auction.

3 Check out as many auctions as possible

Obtain catalogues from as many places as possible and find out if there is a subscription guaranteeing you will be forewarned about upcoming auctions.

Catalogue descriptions may be general and you may need to view the items yourself in order to understand the specifics on what is included in a lot. Judge how promising a sale looks by the large single items on offer. These will generally be described in more detail and will be an indication of what smaller items will be on sale. For example, if there is a lot of Victorian furniture, and several lots of miscellaneous household items and ornaments, then many of these may well be from the same era.

4 Lots of lots

Needless to say, if an item is sold singly and is fully described in the catalogue, there will be more than one person who sees it, and it will sell for market value, so make sure you examine everything that has been included in large groups of items. You may find what you are looking for, and even if this is accompanied by a number of items you don't want, you may always re-sell these to offset your purchase costs.

BOOT FAIRS AND JUMBLE SALES

Boot fairs and jumble sales offer hours of fun in the form of random browsing, as opposed to auctions, which are far more regimented affairs.

But the downside is that there is a lot of junk on offer, in fact, sometimes it is all that is there. At an auction the catalogue will at the very least give you some idea of what treasures might be coming up for sale, but at a boot fair or jumble sale, it is a case of pot luck. So, when shopping at these events for collectibles, consider the following:

1 They are a good source for smaller items

If you are after an original art-deco lounge suite, it is rather doubtful that you will find it at either a boot fair or a jumble sale. Most items on sale will be portable in size.

2 Become a regular

If you find a boot fair or jumble sale which turns up frequent finds make sure you attend as often as possible. Also, talk to stall holders and see if you can figure out why this particular event is so fruitful. It may be that the area was populated by junk shops which have now been killed off by high rents – and the sale participants are the former proprietors - or the area has a high proportion of older people selling their own items in preparation for downsizing to smaller homes.

3 Arrive early and look round thoroughly

The importance of arriving at these events early cannot be overstated. As we have established, good stuff goes quickly and this is especially true of

antiques, collectibles and bargains. Consider setting up a pitch yourself, as this will gain you early entry.

MARKETS, FLEA MARKETS AND COLLECTORS' FAIRS

Traditional markets, specialising as they do in new, cheap produce, are not usually good sources of collectibles or antiques. There are, however, exceptions to this rule:

1 **Look out for 'seconds' on current collectibles**

On occasion, modern collectibles with damaged boxes or other slight flaws wind up on market stalls. These may prove to be bargains. Also watch out for future collectibles. When Dinky Toys became bankrupt in the early 1980s, the final toys made by their factories filtered out through markets, and these are now rare and worth significant amounts of money.

Flea markets and collectors' fairs are another matter. Because they are geared towards trade in antiques and collectibles you are more likely to find more interesting items than you would at a car boot sale. However, you are also more likely to encounter high prices, as traders tend to know more about what they are selling.

2 Look for non-specialist flea market vendors

As with auctioneers, vendors who don't specialise may well under-price the items you are after. Of course, they may also over-price them, so be prepared to haggle. Drop a few salient points of information about the item into the conversation (and make them as downbeat as possible) so they'll think you know more than they do.

3 Take your swaps to swap meets

Take unwanted doubles to swap meets (collectors' fairs) since dealers may be willing to exchange these for items you want. While such transactions usually work in their favour (depending on how cheaply you acquired the items in the first place), it may still cushion the blow on your pocket.

ONLINE SHOPPING

Shopping online for antique/ collectable items produces bargains galore such sites as eBay. The knowledgeable eBay lister will make sure his or her item fetches top dollar, but there are plenty who don't know the value of their items or how to make the system work in their favour.

Remember the following when

HOW TO FIND A BARGAIN

scouring eBay for a bargain collectable:

1 If in doubt, ask

Always use the 'ask vendor a question' button. Never assume anything. Dealing with a vendor whose knowledge is not what it should be may lead to items arriving in a worse condition than promised or turn out to be less-than-rare versions of what you assumed them to be.

2 Never bid early, unless there is a strategic advantage

Vendors are not allowed to change auction text or headlines after a bid is received. If they've misspelt a word in the headline and the opening bid is low, bid quickly to prevent them from correcting the mistake. They may pull the auction, but few will bother. In this way you will prevent the auction from receiving as many hits as it otherwise might and could ensure that it ends with a much lower winning bid. Only go for the opening bid amount when doing this, so as not to drive the price up further. In all other cases, bid as late as possible.

SALES, OUTLET SHOPS AND WAREHOUSE SHOPPING CLUBS

Outlets and warehouse shops can be good places to buy future collectibles cheaply. While neither of these will help to net you a huge bargain in the short term, it may be worth buying several of a single item and putting them away for a few years before selling at a profit. In addition, it is worth remembering that many antique shops now conduct sales. Again, you are unlikely to find any fantastically low prices, but there will be some savings over normal

CARS

Cars which appear to be bargains need thorough checking to make sure they actually are. In many cases, you may find that there is little legal recourse if your bargain vehicle is faulty.

CAR AUCTIONS

Many car auctioneers maintain online businesses, and plenty post information about when and where auctions take place.

There are as many disadvantages to buying a car at auction as there are advantages. It is highly unlikely that you will find a car cheaper, or that you will find a similar variety of vehicles on offer, elsewhere. Also, there are few other places where you will be able to buy a car and have it on the road as quickly. At auctions the paperwork is put through immediately so that you may drive the vehicle home straight away.

It is also highly unlikely that you will have the chance to carry out thorough inspection of prospective purchases. There are no test drives and car auctions can be daunting, as the bidders will mostly be experienced, while the bidding moves at a fast pace. Cars may often be sold in less than a minute. When buying a car at auction:

1 Do your research
Attend as many similar sales as you can before you bid in order to familiarise yourself with the atmosphere and the jargon.

2 Be accompanied by a knowledgeable person
If your knowledge about cars is limited, either take a friend along who does, or pay someone to attend with you. There won't be much of a chance to inspect the vehicles on sale, so it is important to know what to look for in the time you have to check a car over.

3 Stick to your price limit
Not all auction cars are bargains – if two dealers both want the same car and have customers waiting for it, they'll bid against each other and drive the price up, as they'll know they are quickly going to make an immediate

HOW TO FIND A BARGAIN

profit. Don't be tempted to enter into a bidding war.

4 Listen to the dealers

If buying at auction, dealers recommend that you bid for cars that are two to five years old, preferably with full service histories. It is also recommended that you check with the auctioneers that vehicles are guaranteed not to be stolen. If they cannot guarantee this, your car may be taken from you by the former owner's insurance company and you will have no comeback at all.

BOOT FAIRS AND JUMBLE SALES, MARKETS; FLEA MARKETS AND COLLECTORS' FAIRS

Some vendors take the opportunity to put 'For Sale' signs in their vehicles window. While there is no guarantee that these will be bargains, and like any second-hand car, they should be checked out before being bought, they are likely to be cheaper than those bought from dealers. Ensure you check the value with a reputable source.

ONLINE SHOPPING

In the US, eBay Motors has exploded in popularity and currently has tens of thousands of cars for sale. UK eBay doesn't have a separate car section as yet, but there are plenty of cars for sale on the main site.

Often, automobiles are put up for internet auction because owners want to be rid of them quickly and so online sites can be a decent source of bargain-priced vehicles.

However, while many owners will have a genuine reason for listing their cars on eBay, others may well be trying to offload a vehicle that has been troublesome. It is well worth investing in a few of the usual mechanical checks before buying. It is also a good idea to run a check to make sure the car isn't stolen and hasn't been written off. If any owner refuses to allow these checks to be made, under no circumstances should you bid on their vehicle.

If looking for a particular type of older car, it is always an idea to check out the relevant owners' club website. Often these contain classified ads and may prove a good source of well looked-after vehicles.

Going online can often save money on buying a car from abroad. It is a widely known fact that car prices differ across Europe and agencies which previously supplied cars from mainland

Europe by advertising in car magazines now have their own websites.

When buying a car from abroad, remember the following:

1 Check the agency is legitimate

There are plenty of horror stories about people trying to save money by buying through agencies supplying European-sourced cars, and losing a fortune to crooked agents. Make sure whoever you are dealing with is legitimate.

2 Go directly to the dealer
It is possible to order a car from a mainland Europe dealer by going to the manufacturer's website. This way you avoid paying agent fees. However, don't forget to factor in the cost of international telephone calls and transportation for the car.

3 Check where the car you want is cheapest
Monitor online European price surveys to discover the country where your car is cheapest.

4 VAT and insurance
This can be cheaper in the UK

than abroad, so ensure that you pay it here. VAT information may be obtained from www.hmce.gov.uk. The DVLA website will tell you all you need to know about obtaining temporary insurance until the vehicle is officially UK-registered.

5 Japanese and US cars

Plenty of internet agencies supply US-made vehicles which are unavailable in the US, as well as vehicles imported second-hand from Japan.

The Japanese MOT test is so tough to pass that once vehicles there are three years old they are of relatively little value. As the cars are generally still in good condition they are often exported and offer excellent value for money.

Many of these cars are either sports cars or four-wheel-drives which can be cheaper than from a UK dealer. Often, they have automatic transmission and luxury specification fittings which cost extra on UK vehicles.

If you buy directly from one of the agencies in Japan (some of which have online auctions for vehicles), you will

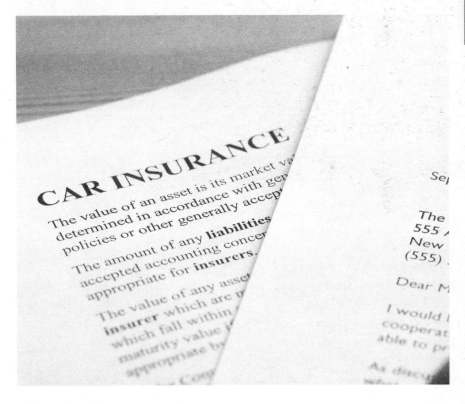

need to arrange the import details and have the car approved for use on British roads by the DVLA. This may involve altering lights, speedometer and various other items. It often works out cheaper to use a UK-based agency, that will supply you with a vehicle that has already been approved for use here.

If you decide to buy an American car, this will almost certainly be left-hand drive, as converting to right hand drive is often prohibitively expensive or impossible to engineer. You will pay more than American consumers, but you can expect the vehicle to hold its value fairly well (especially in the case of sports cars or luxury four-wheel-drives) due to its rarity. So while it may be a trade off of cost against rarity value at purchase time, the vehicle may prove to be more of a bargain when you come to sell it.

SALES AND OUTLET SHOPS

Car dealer sales are always an excellent source of bargains, both new and used, and such events are held as regularly these days as sales at normal shops.

Watch out for adverts in the press, and aim for vehicles which are about to be replaced by new versions in order to achieve the best savings, as dealers will be keen to clear their stock.

In addition to main dealer sales, the UK has now become fair game for US-style 'car supermarkets', which may be classed as 'car outlet' shops. These supply nearly-new or 'as new' cars (usually around one year old with less than ten thousand miles on the odometer). When looking at cars here, shop around, as prices fluctuate between dealers. You can do this online, as many operate websites detailing prices and current stock. As with any nearly-new vehicle purchased either from the UK or abroad, it is also a good idea to check into what warranties are available, and look at the financing options available. Often, car supermarkets offer their own financing schemes, but these are rarely the cheapest option, and shopping around may save a fortune in interest costs.

CLOTHES

Just as collectors relish finding antiques at low prices, fashionistas delight in finding designer label clothes. You can find clothes at most bargain sources.

AUCTIONS
Auctioned clothes fall into the following two categories:

1 Wholesale
Just like any other item, clothing may be left over or part of a liquidation and may end up being sold in bulk lots to the highest bidder.

Lots like this may well include designer names, but will usually be aimed more at vendors, rather than those looking to pick up a couple of pairs of name-brand trousers cheaply. As such, if you are considering buying bulk amounts of clothing, you will doubtless be doing so with an eye to the profits that may be made by reselling. Don't forget, however, that there is the initial outlay of buying, as well as the storage costs and the costs involved in setting up to resell, and that you will need the space to store them all. Be certain that any designer-branded clothing is the real thing, as there are plenty of fakes in circulation.

2 Antique and vintage clothing
Found in lots or as single items, antique or vintage clothing often

makes an appearance at auctions.

Many estate sales include old clothing items, and there are also specific auctions dedicated to more valuable pieces.

The vintage clothing market is one you need to know well in order to obtain bargains. In many cases, the value of an item depends on whether or not it has come back into fashion recently and on personal taste. Also, take into account that vintage examples of some labels are inherently valuable, while others are not. It is certainly not true that all old clothes are worth a fortune and this is especially

the case if they are damaged. Of course, whether an item may be called a bargain or not also depends on what you want it for – if you are planning to wear a particular item of clothing on many occasions, a higher price is justified. Similarly, a collector who buys a piece will justify a price by how much they want the item.

BOOT FAIRS AND JUMBLE SALES

Both boot fairs and jumble sales are excellent sources for bargain clothing.

1 Be prepared to rummage thoroughly

Not all vendors are going to be particularly organised, especially at jumble sales. For every vendor who brings along a foldable coat-rack and has all the clothes they are offering presented neatly on hangers, there'll be another who has a large plastic tub marked 'shirts' with a whole lot of similar items thrown in together. The added bonus of having to hunt for a bargain is that you are more likely to find one. If it is not obvious, then others are less likely to have seen it first.

2 Head for wealthier areas

If you are after second-hand clothes that are expensive when new, then you will stand a good chance of picking up a bargain in these locations.

3 Know your size

It is unlikely that you will be able to try anything on before you buy, so be certain that whatever you are looking at buying will fit properly.

Know what size you are in terms of UK, US and European sizing, and remember that a size 12 in a vintage item may not be the same as standard size 12 today.

4 Check prospective purchases thoroughly

Make sure there is no damage, staining or wear that hasn't been taken into account in the pricing.

HOW TO FIND A BARGAIN

5 Beware of fakes

Always be wary of forgeries when it comes to designer goods. Car boot sales are haunted by rogue traders. If you are looking at a stall that appear to be designer products and the vendor looks like a professional trader, then beware.

MARKETS, FLEA MARKETS AND COLLECTORS' FAIRS

UK markets often include stalls selling various different types of clothing. In a lot of cases, jackets and coats bought at markets may be bargains, as warm, padded jackets and fleeces may be bought far more cheaply than in shops. While quality may, in some cases, not be the best, if you are looking for clothing to wear in a harsh environment such as a workshop or for outdoor work, where it is likely to be damaged, then these may be excellent buys. Markets can also be great places to buy accessories such as gloves, warm hats, scarves and socks cheaply.

As with car boot sales, it is always important to watch out for fake designer goods at markets, as they are another traditional outlet for rogue dealers trading in fake goods. Be wary of market stalls offering Calvin Klein, Ralph Lauren or Tommy Hilfiger products and other designer names as they might be counterfeit goods.

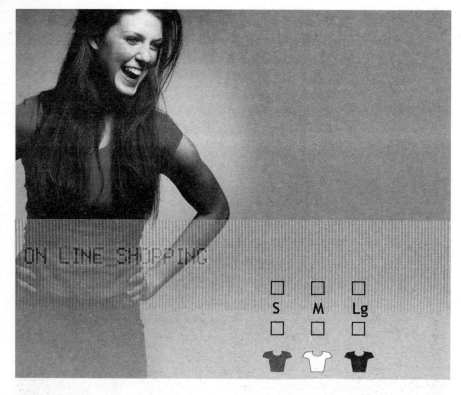

ON LINE SHOPPING

S   M   Lg

ONLINE SHOPPING

There are two major ways of buying clothes online:

1 Online Outlets

More and more designer outlets are moving online. Many of these have plenty of bargains on a wide range of designer clothing for adults and children. Plenty seem to specialise in children's clothes too, which may be a great source of savings for parents. When shopping online, however, do be wary of a few things.

Firstly, make sure you know your size and their returns policy in case the item doesn't fit and it needs to be returned. Secondly, make sure you have a bargain by comparing prices to real life shops, factoring in delivery costs. Finally, ensure you view a picture of the item as large as possible, as colours may vary between a computer screen and real life, and small detail might be missed. Many outlets and designer names are also searchable through comparison search engines which compare prices and find you the best deal.

2 Online auctions

Designer clothing is one of the most popular items for sale on eBay. As with all online auctions, exercise caution when bidding. If you want more images of the item, ask for them. If you decide to bid then win the item, make sure you inspect it as soon as it arrives, and ensure it is as described. If there are any unspecified faults, send it back for a refund or file a complaint with the auction site.

SALES AND OUTLET SHOPS

Both sales and outlet shops offer fantastic savings – as long as you know how to work them.

Obviously, the advantage over buying online is that you have tangible evidence of the quality of the items. However, it is also easier to become carried away on the spur of the moment and buy for the sake of buying, rather than because the item is a bargain. Don't buy goods just because they are cheap, or cheaper than normal. If you fear you will not be able to remain level-headed, then take along an impartial friend who will advise on whether something is a good buy or not.

HOW TO FIND A BARGAIN

Above all, remember the standard tip: arrive as early as possible, preferably before the sale starts, so you know what what the original price is and by how much the price has been reduced. The exception is if you happen to be an unusual size. Chances are the items which will fit you will still be there towards the end of the sale, when prices are often slashed further.

At outlets, scan the rails extensively. These are like boot sales in that you will have to hunt through racks and racks of similar clothing for a real bargain.

WAREHOUSE SHOPPING CLUBS
Many have designer brands although there may not be the variety you require. These are good places to buy basic items such as t-shirts and vests.

COMPUTERS AND SOFTWARE

Computers are similar to cars in that they can cause problems and be expensive if they malfunction and require maintenance.

Second-hand computers can be found in almost any of the circumstances covered by this book: from auctions and car boots to second-hand shops and during the sales. However, while these usually represent significant savings over the price of new equipment, it is not advisable to buy at auction or car boot sales, since there is no provision for you to test before payment.

Computers capabilities expand seemingly by the week – what was cutting-edge two years ago may now not be powerful enough to run the latest software and internet applications. If you want to keep up with technological advances then a newer machine is a must. If, however, you simply want to word-process and print documents, then a second-hand computer may be appropriate.

Buying from a shop specialising in second-hand computers is a good option, as the staff are generally well-informed so should have a reasonable

HOW TO FIND A BARGAIN

idea of what sort of computer will be suitable for your requirements. Many offer warranties on the items they sell.

Alternately, there is a strong trade in second-hand, discounted new and just-out-of-production computers on eBay. As with any purchase made online, read the vendor's description carefully, ask questions before bidding and check the vendor's feedback rating to make sure they are in good standing with other clients.

If you want to purchase a new computer then shop around. Compare prices at online retailers, high street shops and discount electrical shops and look for special offers, such as the inclusion of free printers and free online connectivity. Also, search for products which are newly-discontinued, as these are likely to be powerful enough to meet your requirements and you may be able to buy at a discount. Some retailers carry refurbished machines, which are often sold exclusively through their online stores and these may represent further savings and great value for money as they usually come with warranties comparable to those of new computers.

Warehouse shopping clubs now sell computer equipment, but check prices carefully, as they may not be much cheaper – and are sometimes more expensive – than high street retailers, and equipment such as USB hubs, cords or other computer accessories can usually be purchased cheaper online.

Beware of shop financing and insurance schemes. Financing will usually carry hefty interest payments, as well as plenty of small print in the contract, while extra-to-warranty protection-plan insurance will likely be overpriced and surplus to requirements.

Also consider buying overseas. With a favourable exchange rate and the huge variances in prices from one country to another, buying from abroad can often

produce a bargain, though any goods may be liable to import duty. It may be possible to buy online from retailers in other countries, although many do block foreign buyers.

Buying software second-hand at boot sales and online auctions carries its own risks. You will need to make sure the software isn't out of date or limited to one registered user.

Be very wary of pirated software as often it will not work properly and may even cause expensive and extensive damage to your computer.

When buying a computer always work out in advance what additional software you are likely to need and see if you can find a deal where this is included with the machine you buy. Take advantage of sales, and shop online, as many cyber-retailers offer massive savings and, in many cases, will allow you to download the software directly onto your hard drive, rather than having to wait for the CD-Rom pack to arrive.

You can often pick up free software trials, if it is a demo version you may get a limited version of the program to try out. However, increasingly (especially with new-to-market products), free software trials are complete versions and may last for anywhere from a day to a year. These are available with many useful program

types, including anti-virus software, word processing programs and other internet applications.

Often, there may be several versions of a particular program – a free one with slightly fewer features then another which you have to pay for. In many cases, the free version will be more than adequate for meeting basic requirements.

If the software you require is highly-specialised and is required for your work, it is always worth checking to see if a relevant professional organisation has access to discounts. In many cases unions, guilds and similar trade organisations will negotiate on behalf of their members. This often represents significant savings over the normal purchase price.

ENTERTAINMENT

Entertainment, be it books, music, cinema or theatre tickets, can often be expensive. Fortunately, there are ways to save cash on most varieties of entertainment.

LOYALTY SCHEMES AND SEASON TICKETS

Many cinemas, theme parks, sports stadiums and other venues offer loyalty schemes or season tickets.

Often companies such as mobile phone service providers offer cinema ticket deals as incentives to sign up. When considering a season ticket or cinema loyalty scheme, read the fine print and make sure you will use the venue often enough to justify the expense. Similarly, when choosing a mobile phone provider, don't be swayed by free offers if the phone service is not suitable for your needs.

There are numerous other loyalty-card schemes operating, especially in major cities. These offer discounts to cardholders in return for promotion on the card's website. If you routinely visit several places for entertainment, or which are in your immediate area, then it may be a worthwhile exercise.

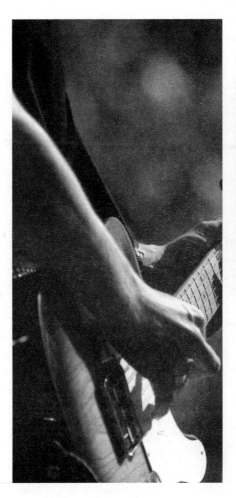

LIVE EVENTS

The key to avoiding the high prices for live event tickets is to make sure you know ahead of time when particular shows are occurring. For theatre and pop concerts, keep abreast of official websites and buy tickets as soon as they go on sale. When booking through an agency, you will pay a commission on the ticket.

Theatre tickets are often cheaper for mid-week and Saturday matinees.

NON-LIVE ENTERTAINMENT

Besides cinema loyalty schemes, there are other ways to buy reduced price tickets. As with the theatre, going to a matinee on a weekday may make prices cheaper. Also, if there is ever anything wrong with the cinema; it hasn't been cleaned, for example, it is always worth politely pointing this out to the manager. Often, this will result in your being offered another visit for free.

The cinema isn't the only place filmed entertainment costs money – buying and renting videos and DVDs may also be expensive. As such, make sure you shop around for the best rental deals. Often, high street shops don't offer the best prices. These often may be found online, with websites that post you the DVD you require, along with a postage-paid envelope for you to return it to them. Usually, there is no extra fee for however long you keep the DVD either. And don't forget to check out the local library as many stock films and music, although unlike books, there will usually be a nominal rental charge for films or music. The technologically inclined may also want to check out the new websites that allow you to legally download films or

music to your computer, as these may be cheaper.

If you prefer to buy your DVDs, CDs or books rather than rent then it is best to compare prices online to see which is the most competitive. Prices for new books may often be cheaper online – the online store Amazon very often offers books at discounted rates.

Alternatively, check out boot sales, jumble sales or anywhere else where second-hand items are sold. Do bear in mind, however, that these may be damaged, so make sure the price is reduced accordingly.

A much better bet are specialist second-hand CD/DVD shops, as these usually test items before they go on sale. Many will also do buyback schemes where you may sell them your old CDs or DVDs and receive money off further purchases. Books may be bought or sold in similar shops, or borrowed free from libraries, and have the added bonus that you buy them safely from any source of used goods, as it is easier to tell if they are damaged or not.

Finally, if you do find a good second-hand CD/DVD shop, remember that if you are likely to watch a film more than once, you may be better off buying it there than renting it again, as rental fees soon add up. And you can always sell it if you choose to later.

UTILITY SERVICES

Like food, furniture and household items, utility services – telephone, gas, electricity, water – represent a constant outlay of cash.

Electricity, gas and water

Electricity, gas and to a lesser extent, water can usually be provided by various companies, so it pays to shop around. Don't stay with the same provider just because you've been with them for years. Comparison-shop to see which company is cheapest and switch if someone else can offer you lower bills. Use the internet to create a list of the providers in your area, then check out their websites or contact call centres to receive pricing details. Don't be swayed by special offers from power, or any other, companies offering incentives like free cable TV connection to switch suppliers, unless the actual fees for the core service are cheaper. And always check contract lengths, as you don't want to be locked in to one provider for any longer than you absolutely have to be.

Telephone, internet and mobile phone services

Landline services are similar to electricity and gas, in that it can be provided by numerous companies and you may shop around to save cash.

When doing this, it is a good idea to work out what you use your phone for – local calls, repeated calls to the same numbers or international calls and look for a good deal which will offer you the best pricing on these. Read all the small print as many of the 'special offers' that give for example, cheap international calls, will make up for this by high prices on regular calls, and this may negate any potential bargain.

Also, see what internet service options are available, since many internet providers may only offer connectivity through certain phone line providers – and if you use any others, you may have to switch to their internet service. This may well be more expensive, and if you are in the middle of a contract with your current internet service provider, you may end up paying both subscriptions even though you will only use one.

Always shop around as much as possible when looking for an internet service provider, and compare all prices and special offers.

If buying broadband, look for offers that give you a free modem, or opt not to buy the modem pack offered by the company, since broadband modems are usually available at a cheaper price from electrical shops or online retailers.

Mobile phone tariffs are another area

where prices vary greatly. They may be ruinously expensive if you choose the wrong one, so always shop around when looking for a new plan. Discuss with the shop staff whether pay-as-you-go, contract plans or the newly-available mixture plans will be best for you and don't be swayed by free add-ons like video or picture messaging if you won't ever use them. Always keep an eye on your bill. If you find yourself constantly going over your allocation of free minutes or text messages, arrange to switch to another tariff. Most companies are flexible about this (as long as you want more minutes, not less), and it is almost always better to pay a higher monthly rate than it is to pay excess call charges.

Always check contract lengths, and

aim to be signed up to one particular company for as short a space of time as possible, since this will give you more flexibility. At the end of your contract, don't immediately re-sign; check elsewhere to see if you can find a better deal, and then see if your current company will match or better it.

Also consider the handsets you will receive by switching, as you will often have the option of several to choose from for free, or at least for a knock-down price. You can always sell your old one to cover, or help towards, the cost. Alternately, you may have your old one unlocked, and see if you can receive further cash incentives for not being given a new handset.

FOOD

When you think of items you may buy at bargain prices, food doesn't come at the top of the list, and buying it cheaply must be done with care, as food that is past is use-by date or is otherwise contaminated may be highly detrimental to your health. That said, there are still several ways to make savings when buying food.

AUCTIONS

Despite popular preconceptions, food is sold at auction. Farmers sell produce to retailers at auction, and long-life food or freeze-dried items are often sold in bulk at auctions of surplus stock.

Needless to say, both of these are geared more towards the vendor than the immediate consumer, particularly the produce auctions, as this sort of

foodstuff doesn't have a long shelf-life. However, if you have a particular liking for long-life foods and plenty of space to store them, buying numerous crates at auction can be a great saving.

MARKETS

UK markets often feature stalls offering food for sale and often a lot of it is very reasonably priced.

For the most part, market stalls sell either foodstuffs that don't spoil quickly, like biscuits and cakes, or fresh vegetables and fruit.

Often, baked goods, sweets, cakes and biscuits bought from market stalls may be far cheaper than they would be in the shops. However, the vast majority of these products are not name-brand produce, and as such may not taste quite the same as the brand you are used to, so if you are a particularly fussy eater, you may prefer to stick to the supermarket. Also, be sure to check sell-by dates, as you don't want to be buying out-of-date food.

The fresh produce sold at markets may not always be cheaper than buying in supermarkets, as supermarkets may pile it high and sell it cheap, while market traders have different overheads. However, as with most things, it pays to shop around, as you may well find some things are cheaper, while others are more expensive. Farmers markets may also offer organic produce and other foodstuffs, and while these will generally be as expensive as the equivalent shop-sold items, they may often be fresher.

ONLINE SHOPPING

While online supermarket shopping has taken off recently, it hardly ever offers bargains. There is usually a delivery fee of around £5, and if an item is out of stock it may be substituted with a similar item. You will also miss out on any specials and in-store price cuts that may not be advertised on the shop websites.

WAREHOUSE SHOPPING CLUBS

Warehouse shopping clubs are by far the best places to buy food at bargain prices.

You will need to buy in bulk to make the biggest savings and do remember that all that food will have to be stored somewhere so think about the amount of storage space you have at home. And, if you don't have a car transporting it home may be difficult.

Also, remember to check use-by dates, as you don't want food to go off before you can use it, as this will negate the lower price you paid for it in the first place.

Finally, it is a good idea to remember to buy a variety of items. Just because one product has extra money off the already cut-price, doesn't mean you should necessarily load-up with twice as much. A huge glut of any one item may mean half of it ends up going to waste.

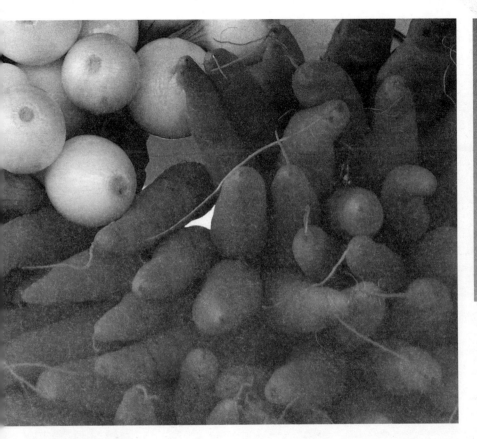

LOYALTY SCHEMES

Most supermarkets run loyalty schemes, usually offering points for the amount spent and vouchers for money off in return. These may help make savings, but watch out, as many of these schemes are not as helpful as they first seem. Often, the schemes require you to use a loyalty card which is swiped at the checkout. The supermarket may then track what you buy and will send money-off vouchers for similar, more expensive products in the hope that once you have tried these once, you will stick to them, and spend more money. When your coupons arrive in the post, go through them carefully and bin any that are for products you wouldn't normally buy, or which are only for large amounts of products that you won't use. Make sure and use the ones that are directly redeemable for money off your overall bill though – these really are useful.

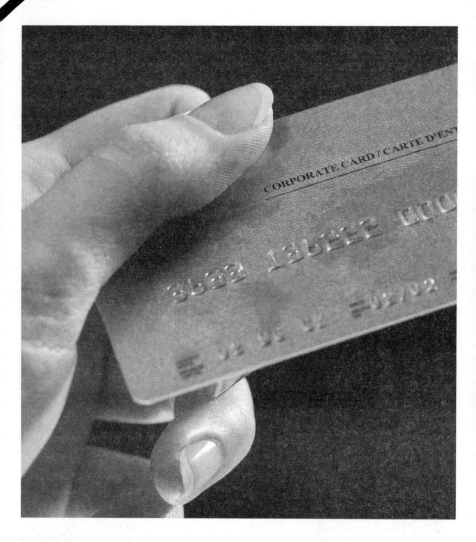

FINANCIAL PRODUCTS

Many bargains, particularly cars or property, require finance to enable you to purchase them. Similarly, a credit or debit card is a necessity when shopping online, so you need to make sure you find the best deal possible when shopping for either one of these. A loan or credit card with a high interest rate may swiftly wipe out the advantage gained by hunting out whatever bargain it is you've found. Similarly, make sure that you keep your money in an account which will guarantee you the most interest. That way, when you find bargains, you will have more to spend on them.

By far the best place to look for good deals on all financial products is the internet. All major banks and financial institutions have websites, with details of all the services they offer in terms of loans, credit cards or accounts. There are also many advice sites which will offer quick comparison tables of cards, loans or mortgages, showing which establishments offer the best deals in terms of interest rates, repayment term lengths and balance transfers.

When using these sites, it is a good idea to check the comparison tables offered by several similar sites since, as with search engines, some may favour the products of 'partner' sites who have advertising deals with them. It is also a good idea to keep checking back at regular intervals to see if deals have changed. Often, financial institutions phase out old accounts and bring in new ones in their place, and you may find that moving your money elsewhere makes more sense. In addition, you may well find that online-only banks and services offer higher interest rates on accounts and better deals on loans, since they don't have the overheads associated with having physical high street branches.

FURNITURE AND HOUSEHOLD GOODS

There are many good sources for finding furniture and household goods at bargain prices.

AUCTIONS

Auctions are a rich source of furniture and other household goods. While antique pieces range from expensive to badly-damaged, newer pieces can often be bought at non-specialist antique auctions for very low prices. And unlike many items sold at auction, cars, for example, viewing furniture before the sale will usually show up any problems.

The exceptions to this rule are electrical items, not least because potential danger accompanies any faults.

Smaller household items such as lamps, ornaments and bric-a-brac may also be found at auctions, with prices varying greatly depending on what you are looking at and the type of auction.

BOOT FAIRS AND JUMBLE SALES

These are an excellent source of smaller homeware items, although again, with electrical pieces, care needs to be taken as there is little means of redress if they don't work. Anything bought here should be inspected for wear, as there is

HOW TO FIND A BARGAIN

usually a reason why something has been donated or is being sold and it may not just be that the owner has grown tired of it.

You tend not to find larger pieces of furniture such as sideboards and three-piece-suites at jumble or car boot sales, although there are the odd exceptions to this rule. Don't forget, though, that you will have to transport your purchase home – usually immediately – which might be difficult to arrange at short notice unless you have a large vehicle at your disposal.

MARKETS, FLEA MARKETS AND COLLECTORS' FAIRS

UK markets often sell smaller homeware items at knockdown prices. When buying these, inspect for quality.

Flea markets can be a fabulous source for old furniture and household items. Furniture pieces found here can be in poor condition. While this is good news for the amateur restorer, consider the potential costs and whether or not you have the skills required.

Nevertheless, for many highly valuable antique items, buying damaged and restoring may be the only option for those on a budget.

ONLINE SHOPPING

When purchasing furniture without actually seeing and measuring it, extra care always needs to be taken. Colours may differ greatly and exact measurements should be checked, since digital images may distort perceptions of size. Usually with an online order, the items must be delivered directly to your home and may not be collected from a shop. It is always worth checking to see if the company offers free delivery as an option. This may take a couple of days longer than standard delivery. If you have a suitable vehicle however, and the online price is the same as the shop price, then you may want to purchase from the shop and collect yourself.

Increasingly, vendors using online auctions are selling larger items such as suites, sofas and other furniture items. Smaller household goods are already an eBay staple and may be purchased at excellent prices.

Bargains are also available on larger pieces of furniture, but if possible these should always be viewed before purchasing in order to verify condition. And as vendors will mostly be private individuals, you will probably have to make your own arrangements for collection.

SALES, SECOND-HAND, CHARITY AND OUTLET SHOPS

During sales, furniture is often greatly reduced in price as it generally takes up a lot of in-store space. Deals may also often be improved should you opt for ex-display pieces, as these are usually the very last items left, although check fully for faults and wear.

Second-hand and charity shops specialising in furniture are filled with bargains. The latter type are now opening in ever greater numbers, as charity shops diversify, selling good quality items at rock-bottom prices, since the items are donated. Generally, electrical items are all tested.

WAREHOUSE SHOPPING CLUBS

Warehouse shopping clubs often offer household items at wholesale prices. Since these are not the staple products of such retailers, shop around because they may not necessarily be that much cheaper than elsewhere.

ITEMS FOR RESALE

Selling is covered in detail in a later chapter, but for now, here are some good places to buy bargain items you may resell at a profit.

Items for resale fall into two categories:

Items bought in bulk/wholesale

This is when you buy a large number of identical items, with the intention of selling them on singularly and making a profit in the process.

Single items

These are items you see at a low price, and buy with the intention of selling in another marketplace at a higher price.

AUCTIONS

These can be an excellent source of wholesale goods. Many items which are unwanted, as a result of over-stocking or company liquidation, are sold at auction, and as such, there are fantastic buys on items which are split up and sold singly. With this type of deal, however, it is important to be expert in what you are buying, and how you are going to sell it on, as well as having the right transport and storage.

Auctions are a good source for single items to sell on at a profit. Many antique dealers buy stock which they then mark-up and sell on in their shops. Do consider that, if you've outbid a professional dealer, then you probably

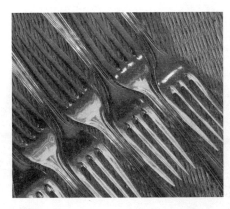

are not going to make a huge profit by selling it on.

BOOT FAIRS AND JUMBLE SALES

You often find single items that can be sold on elsewhere for higher prices. This really depends on the market for a particular item. As we will see later, items need to be sold in the right market to achieve their full price potential.

MARKETS, FLEA MARKETS AND COLLECTORS' FAIRS

At flea markets and collectors' fairs you will generally find single items to sell on, but as you will usually be buying from more knowledgeable vendors, not so much of a source of bargains, unless you are lucky.

ONLINE SHOPPING

With auctioneers taking to the web in increasing numbers, offering everything from cars to computers through their

own auction sites, shopping online is now a sizeable source of wholesale stock.

In terms of single items bought to sell on, there are always opportunities to acquire items at less than their actual value on online auction sites, and then sell these on immediately at a profit.

There is also the opportunity to make a good profit out of entertainment events by buying tickets to these online as soon as they go on sale, and then putting them up for sale at a premium after the event has sold out.

SALES, SECOND-HAND, CHARITY AND OUTLET SHOPS

Sales are a rich source of single items, especially if the savings are big and the items hard to find. Not everyone will be physically in the area to buy at the sale, and those who cannot find anything similar will often be interested in buying, in many cases at the original price.

WAREHOUSE SHOPPING CLUBS

As these initially started out as venues for retailers to buy wholesale, they remain an excellent source of resale items, in terms of bulk stocks of food and household products. If selling you will, of course, need to ensure you have suitable storage for the products and all the legalities are in place for you to sell perishable foodstuffs. Failure to meet hygiene standards can result in severe penalties.

PROPERTY

With property prices climbing, the allure of finding a house or flat at a bargain price has never been greater. However, supposed bargains should be approached with extreme care; fixing the hidden horrors in a house can be extremely costly.

The most obvious way is simply to haggle with the estate agent or vendor. Make a list of all the negative points about your prospective purchase and obtain quotes on how much these will cost to fix. Then add a little more for the annoyance factor, deduct this from the price and make your offer. Don't be afraid to put in a low offer but make sure you view as many properties as possible, since this way you may be able to play vendors off against each other.

If you are DIY-savvy, target properties which require work. But obtain a survey by a professional if you are unsure as to whether or not fixing the property is beyond your capabilities. And check that the cost of renovation will not eat into all of your profit if your plan is to re-sell.

It is always wise to shop for property during the autumn and winter as they tend to be slower months. Making a low offer just before Christmas increases your chances of having it accepted as the vendors may not relish the prospect of waiting until spring for another to come along.

Property auctions may offer substantial bargains, but usually only to those who know what they are doing. It is true that property sold at auction generally goes for lower values than those achieved by haggling with the estate agent. However, when you buy at an auction, there is usually no opportunity for building surveys. Even the most competent DIY expert is not able to gauge the true condition of a structure by the cursory look-over granted prior to auction.

It is this which makes buying from an estate agent a safer bet. That is, unless you possess surveying skills or know someone who does. With any auction, there is always an element of risk involved. With a property auction, the risk is that much greater – although when it goes right, so are the rewards.

These days buying a property abroad offers more opportunities for bargains. Prices are generally lower and exchange rates may also be beneficial. There are several necessary steps to be taken when buying abroad:

1 Location

Are you planning on living in the property full time? If so, do your homework. Find the right place geographically for you and your family, taking into account jobs, schools, lifestyle and all the other aspects of day-to-day life. The region may be cheaper, but will salaries be lower? What about language barriers? Will you feel at home there? Always make sure you've visited and like the place you intend to move to well enough to set up home there and remember that being on holiday somewhere isn't the same as living there. Also take into account moving costs, you may find your costs are very high if you decide you want to leave after a year or so.

If you are buying to rent, either as a holiday home or on a permanent basis,

check out the region and make sure there are prospective tenants. Investigate your rights and responsibilities as landlord, since these may vary from country to country. In addition, invest in professional advice on your British tax and legal status.

2 **Use a reputable estate agent**
For any one country there are plenty of estate agencies on the internet bidding for your business, if possible, choose by word of mouth rather than on the basis of the agency's own assertions.

3 **Approach timeshare schemes with caution**
Or at least look into them with extreme caution. Many of these schemes purport to offer you use of a property in an exotic location for part of the year, but are often little more than rip-offs and certainly not the bargains they seem to be. Check that the vendor is a member of a professional organisation and read the small print carefully if you are considering buying into one, as you may well end up paying hefty subscription fees with little prospect of return.

TRAVEL AND HOTELS

With countless television programmes about holidays from hell, the image of bargain travel has taken something of a bashing. However, the advent of the internet combined with fierce competition in the holiday market to create a wealth of genuine bargains and the careful consumer can save a fortune while travelling.

When shopping for air tickets, hotels or car rental deals, it pays to use one of the many excellent websites dedicated to providing these services. Usually they may offer large discounts and there is the added convenience of taking care of every aspect simultaneously.

The key to these websites is to book as early as possible – prices increase considerably the closer you are to the departure date. Use the 'hold' function to reserve seats at the current price for however long the individual site allows. If the prices go up in the meantime, and you then decide to buy, you may attain the earlier, cheaper price. Be warned, however, that most sites will only let you hold for 24 to 48 hours.

As with all internet shopping, always shop around. Compare prices for the same bookings, as they vary. When buying plane tickets, check the prices with the carrier. On rare occasions, they are cheaper, especially if you are booking close to the date when you want to travel.

While booking late decreases your chances of finding an internet flight bargain, it may increase your chances of finding a holiday bargain through a travel agent. When the holiday season peaks, last-minute breaks are reduced to fill places. Be aware that this greatly reduces the chance of finding exactly the destination you want.

When shopping through a travel agent – last minute or not – it maybe a good idea to book a package, or have them arrange car hire and accommodation at the same time as flights. Again, shop around and you may be able to play agents off against each other in terms of the discounts or

added benefits. The internet is also a good place to shop for complete breaks, as all the major travel agencies now have websites – and even Ceefax and Teletext still advertise bargains.

Also, look for holiday destinations closer to home; many will be running special offers to attract local holidaymakers.

One final word of warning: holidays that are so cheap that they seem too good to be true usually are. Find out what your hotel or resort looks like in advance by browsing brochures or official websites. Then if it doesn't match up exactly, don't be afraid to complain loudly as this will almost always achieve some form of compensation.

SELLING ON
AT A PROFIT

For the most part, bargains fall into two categories: goods you need and items which are too much of a good deal to resist buying.

The latter category offers a world of opportunities for selling on at a profit. It is almost inevitable that once you start bargain-hunting you will want to fund your activities in this way as a means of generating extra income. However, selling for profit can be tricky; after all, as a bargain hunter you don't want to be seen to be offering bargains yourself.

of information on any given product or subject. Check out the 'completed auctions' search function on eBay, which provides inside info on the prices raised by similar items. Visit your local library, or consult an expert.

Impartial advice is always the best advice. Try and obtain information from two or more sources. For example, consult both the internet and an auction house expert, as different items may be better suited to different markets, both in terms of how and where you sell.

KNOW YOUR MARKET

There may be no demand for a certain type of collectible in the UK, but plenty of call for it in another country – this is where research will come into play. If this is the case, either list it with an auctioneer who has a global clientele or sell via an online body such as eBay.

KNOW YOUR PRODUCT

It is important have as much knowledge as possible about whatever you are selling. Perhaps you have some collectibles that you bought in a lot but you aren't knowledgeable about them. it is important that you research the products before you even think about selling them on.

The internet has made this so much easier. Search engines access a wealth

WHERE TO SELL?

Places, like auction houses, in which you sell will have costs to the vendor. It is important to work out how much to spend in relation to how much an individual item will fetch.

AUCTIONS

Many auctioneers offer free valuations but they take a percentage of whatever the item sells for, their values may often

tend to be optimistic. As always, search out more than one opinion.

If your item is unusual, in good condition or both, you may be advised by the auctioneers to wait for a specialist auction which may possibly gain you a higher price. Consider placing a reserve price on it, this amount is decided with the help of the auction house. When setting reserves, be realistic; if pitched too high, the reserve will put potential bidders off.

If your item doesn't fetch its value, consider selling anyway as the alternative may well cost you. Many auction houses charge a fee on unsold goods to cover their costs and you may end up taking your item home but still having to pay a charge. The amount charged in unsold fees varies between auction houses and depends on the item being auctioned. For lower-value items at smaller auction houses, a flat fee of approximately £8 to £10 is the norm. Other auctioneers may use a percentage structure to calculate the fee. If you are considering selling at auction, you should most definitely ask about this upfront.

Commission on sales is between 10%–15% of the final hammer price. There are costs relating to insurance, storage and handling charges, as well as a photography fee if your item is featured in the auction catalogue. All of these will be subject to VAT. Make sure you obtain a list of all of charges up front and factor them alongside the assessor's valuation of your item. Only then will you know whether your item is appropriate for auction.

CAR BOOT FAIRS

Car boot fairs offer ideal opportunities for selling portable items such as household goods, books, clothes and DVDs, although always make sure to check retail values to ensure that a collectible isn't going to slip out of your hands for just a few pennies. When it comes to larger items, be aware that failure to sell will result in you having to take them home.

When selling at a car boot fair, it is important to sort your items by type, ensure that you mark prices clearly and work out how much of a reduction you are willing to make on pieces priced at

SELLING ON AT A PROFIT

more than a few pounds. Take two folding tables and a cash box. Bags and packing material will be appreciated by your buyers.

You will need to book and pay for your pitch at the sale ground, this will be around £10-£15, depending on the size of your vehicle and whether you are a private seller or professional trader. Factor in the cost of petrol, stationery for marking prices and folding tables.

SECOND-HAND SHOPS

Target the second-hand shops which specialise in the relevant items you have for sale.

Second-hand shops operate on one of two principles. Some sell items on a commission or return basis, whereby they offer the item in their shop for a set period of time and take a percentage commission if it sells, or return it to you if they don't find a buyer. More commonly, others buy items outright and sell on at a profit.

The former will be more profitable, but the main drawback is that you are not paid immediately and there is always the possibility that your item will not sell at all. The latter is a source of ready cash, but it is likely that you will receive less than half of the resale value. In the cases of shops specialising in entertainment products like second hand DVDs and CDs, many will have a 'standard' price scheme for what they offer per DVD or CD, this may be 50p or £1 per copy which they will sell on from upwards of £5.

When selling items such as clothes,

always take a few items as one lot. Shops will often turn their nose up at one or two items, or offer a lower price, as it is a hassle to process just a few items at once. Take too many and they may try to offer you a lower price by offering a 'lot' price which is less than if the items are sold individually.

SECOND-HAND AND ANTIQUE DEALERS

While these operate on the buy-and-resell principle, the term 'dealer' applies mostly to resellers of items such as cars and antiques.

When selling to a dealer, do research beforehand. Second-hand shops generally have a hard and fast rule

about how much they pay for items in relation to how much they sell them on for.

Make the item you are selling as attractive as possible. If it is a car, clean it, if it is an antique then make sure it is thoroughly presentable. Know your product and be knowledgeable when speaking to the expert so they are aware that you understand the item's true value. In some cases, particularly with cars, many dealers offer part-exchange, where they will buy your vehicle, usually along with cash, in

exchange for another, newer car. If considering this make sure there isn't another way you could get a better deal – by selling privately, for example.

PRIVATE ADVERTISEMENTS

There is now a proliferation of small ad opportunities, from dedicated papers such as *Loot* and specialist magazines like *Auto Trader* to notice boards in supermarkets, the back pages of local papers to the huge variety of specialist and general online listings.

Although they tend to be hit-and-miss, small ads can be very useful when it comes to selling. Consider how valuable your item is as this will dictate the venue and size of your advertisement. There is no need to take out an advertisement in a national magazine to sell an item that's worth £50, but with a car that may be worthwhile. If the item is rare, or will be of interest to a specific group of people, advertise in a place they are likely to visit.

For example, a classic car would be best advertised in an owners' club magazine, while nursery furniture should be sold through the free notice board of a local community centre that has a Sunday crèche.

The cost of a classified advertisement

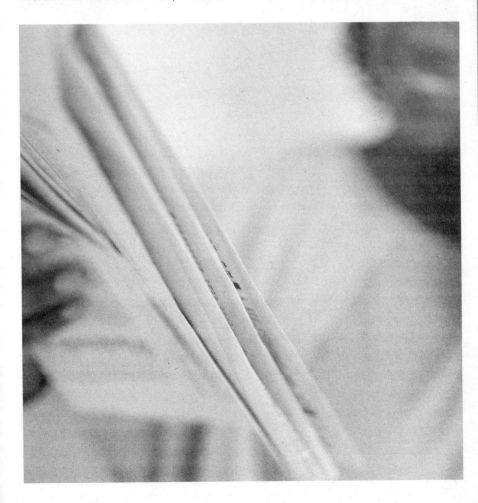

SELLING ON AT A PROFIT

varies depending on where you place it. In an ad-only paper like *Loot*, or a national or local newspaper the cost varies depending on the size and run of the advertisement. Some will offer a short run for free, but if you want it to appear for more than a couple of days you will have to pay. Most charge a flat fee for a certain number of words, then add to the cost for each word you go over the limit. Sales features such as impact lines and bold text can cost more. As a rule of thumb the smaller the paper's circulation, the cheaper the ad will be.

Look out for advertising packages, where your ad is placed in the print publication as well as online for a flat fee. Again, this varies depending on the publication, but for a popular magazine and website such as UK *Autotrader*, prices start at around £27 - always try and haggle with magazines and newspapers to get a discount.

As for print advertisements, consider including a picture with a listing for a high-value item, or paying extra for bold typeface or impact lines to make your item stand out.

Be as accommodating as possible to would-be buyers when arranging viewings and make sure your item is clean and complete. Place untraceable contact information, such as a mobile number or a disposable internet-based email address, instead of say, your landline phone number.

SELLING ONLINE

The internet is an excellent selling tool; there is the opportunity to reach buyers worldwide, which can make you an excellent return.

The two main ways of selling online is via auction or classifieds.

ONLINE AUCTIONS

By far the most popular way for individuals to sell online is through eBay or a similar auction sites such as eBid or uk-floggit.com. These are simple to use; you choose a username and register through the online system. Registering to sell will require that you have a valid credit or debit card on file, in order that the auctioneers can be assured of collecting the fees they charge for selling. Hence, you will need to make sure you have a card which is one of the varieties they take, as some

will not accept Switch/Solo or other debit cards.

While bidders at regular auctions can personally view an item, online bidders cannot. As such, you will need to make sure they see pictures of the item since auctions with no photographs are more unlikely to achieve close to the true value of the item. A digital camera, the higher resolution the better or a scanner is therefore a necessity. eBay and most other auction sites will allow you to upload photographs through their system, but most charge extra for more than one picture per auction. Therefore, if you have your own server, consider uploading your photos there, and

SELLING ON AT A PROFIT

having a link to them, as this will be free. As with regular auctioneers, most online auction sites charge commission on the winning bid price for whatever you sell. Commission usually begins at around 5% for a low value item and will rise to around 9% for a high value piece.

There is also a listing fee and this will increase depending on how high you set the start price. Optional features for your auction include bold text auction headings, reserve prices, advertisement on the site's homepage, and will also carry additional fees. The fees for these vary depending on the feature. A gallery listing picture, where a photograph of your item appears in the search results, will cost just a few pence, while an appearance on the site's homepage can be as much as £50.

Fee structures for high-value special items like cars or property may be different. All auction sites contain details of their fee structures in their 'help' sections, along with guidelines on using the optional, extra-cost features. They offer online tools for bulk sellers, where items may be listed either on auction or at fixed prices with lower fees incurred, that won't be included in the searches bidders run on the main site.

Research your items thoroughly using the 'completed auctions search' function. This will give you an idea on how a particular item will sell or not, and for how much. It will also indicate whether or not you should sell as part of a lot or separately. Look at auctions which achieve highest prices and note the category and what key-words are in the heading to be found by buyers. Make a note of these and use similar words when writing your own auction heading and text.

Be sure to describe any item in as much detail as possible, noting good points and any faults (this will help to avoid buyers returning items and demanding their money back). Answer questions from potential bidders as promptly as possible and despatch the item quickly to ensure you get good feedback. If you are selling in volume, consider using a 'shop', or any of the other bulk-selling tools. These will make it easier to keep track of your sales.

Certain companies such as the UKs auctioning4u and DropShop in

Germany have 'drop-off' points where you can deposit items that they will sell on auction sites on your behalf. The advantage is that they employ experts who make sure listings are written to maximise sales potential, take and upload high-resolution pictures and handle elements such as collection of payment, packaging and post. Most charge a fee of around 30% of the final value of an item, but as listings with multiple photographs and full descriptions are more expensive, this should offset the added cost. These companies usually operate a minimum value for items they will accept. This varies between companies, but in the UK it is generally £20.

ONLINE CLASSIFIEDS

There are dozens of websites around the world offering goods via online classified advertising such as, loot.com, exchangeandmart.co.uk and adtrader.com. When considering selling through one of these sites do consider the nature of the item you are selling and pick a site where the most potential buyers will see it.

A general-use item will probably sell well on any of the big ad sites, but a specialist item may have less of a market there. If it's an antique or collectable item, you may prefer to look for a website aimed at those who are interested in this particular item.

The cost of placing online classified

adverting varies widely depending on where you place them, and what sort of ad you want. A small, specialist site with a classifieds section may place ads for free. Even some of the larger sites, such as *Loot*, carry the ad for a two-day period. Photographs, bold text and impact boxes cost extra. Prices for these vary between sites and depend on whether or not you can obtain a package deal.

Get your advertisement on the website and in the advertiser's print paper publication for a one-off cost, which often includes extra features like pictures and bold text within the price. *Exchange and Mart's* exchangeandmart.com's car advertisements start at around £9 for a three-week, online-only ad, but go up to £76 for an integrated, internet-and-publication package which remains advertised until the vehicles is sold.

With so many options available, it is a matter of researching as many sites as possible to get the right environment for selling your item.

If, for example, a nearly-new car is selling for just under the price it was bought for, you will have enough margin to place a more expensive ad with a photograph. If the sale item is an old car selling for £500, stick to a cheaper advertisement service. Sites also run special promotions which offer discounts on advertisement space, so shop around.

Higher volume vendors should consider setting up their own website. The most expensive is a dedicated website, designed by a professional designer specifically for your business, while the easiest to create will be a shop in an online mall. With these you sign up, put your product details into their shop template, upload pictures and are ready to go. When calculating the cost and effectiveness of having your own website, however, take into account the size of your business, turnover and revenue. You will need to be able to accept credit card payments, and to do this must either sign up for a special merchant account, authorise a payment processing company to accept payments on your behalf, or open your shop in an online mall, where the mall will accept payments on your behalf.

Merchant accounts are the cheapest way of accepting credit cards and malls the most expensive, but a merchant account is suitable for a larger, high-revenue business which qualifies under the stringent regulations. Mall shops are the most expensive way to accept cards since the mall itself will require a percentage of each transaction in addition to monthly or yearly 'shop rental' fees.

Online payment systems like PayPal may also be used by businesses to receive credit card payments. Fees here are around 2.5% per transaction.

You will need a well-designed website, which has the capability to accept credit card payments. Systems such as PayPal are becoming increasingly popular with one-man online businesses but always make sure you trade via a secure server which is safe for customers to enter credit card details. Other factors to consider include: site maintenance, regular updating of content and the ability to pack and ship items.

BUYING TO RESELL

Each of the following areas has its pros and cons:

1 Buying wholesale

Always ensure you can resell your bulk-purchased items singularly and thus make a profit. When researching your market, find out where you will be selling, the size of the market, the scale of the margins for single and bulk items and how long it will take to shift them all.

Make sure you have sufficient storage and transport capabilities. Quantities of even the smallest items still take up space and require large vehicles to carry them from point of purchase to point of storage. All this costs money, so make sure you factor the costs of these into your calculations.

Consider the other overheads. Will you have to pay rent for a shop to sell through? Or for a regular pitch at a car boot sale? If you are selling food or other perishable goods, will you need a special licence? And will you need to register as a trader for taxation purposes? Make sure you find out all of the above, and know the respective costs of each.

2 Buying a single item for resale

If you are buying a single item with the intent to resell it at a profit, the likelihood is that it will be an antique, collectible or an item you can achieve a sizeable profit on in another market. For example, you may buy antique china at a car boot sale then resell it at auction. Alternatively, you might attend a sale at a designer clothing shop, then list the items online to sell to someone in a market where there is no access to this label or particular item.

It is best to stick to whatever arena of collecting you have the most experience and knowledge about, as this is where you will be able to spot items that will be profitable to resell.

Consider the following bargain categories in order to maximise returns.

ANTIQUES AND COLLECTIBLES

Specialist auctions provide a relevant audience for more valuable collectibles, but remember the auctioneers fees and commission. While these are suitable for high-value goods, lower-value items will probably sell better online, where there is a wider audience.

CARS

Advertising a car for sale privately

through classifieds, either in a targeted magazine or newspaper or online, is generally the best way to sell your car. Selling to a dealer scores lower prices, although smart negotiators may be able to bargain for a beneficial part-exchange deal.

CLOTHES

For non-designer items still in good condition try car boot sales and for mint condition designer items and baby clothes online auctions are a better prospect. There are sale-on-consignment clothing specialists, such as London's Insight Agency and Butterfly Agency where you can offload specialist items such as bridal gowns. These will draw the clientele looking for such specific items.

COMPUTERS AND SOFTWARE

Computers sell well through small advertisements, where you can target buyers directly. Many computer shops

will buy used systems for resale, but only at prices which will give them a profit. Some may allow for part-exchange. If your equipment is in good condition and you have a high trust rating, selling online at auction is advisable, especially with nearly-new items which still have warranties.

ENTERTAINMENT

Unless the film, book or CD is rare and sought-after, the likelihood is that you won't make a profit on your used home-entertainment items. You can, however, obtain a return by selling at car boot sales, or by taking to a specialist second-hand shop. Selling online at auction is also a possibility, although there are low returns on second-hand mass-market items. Large lots of similar items may sell for more.

Online auctions are by far the best place to offload unwanted concert or event tickets, as these can often recoup the initial cost and sometimes even turn a profit if the event is sold out or in demand.

FURNITURE AND HOUSEHOLD ITEMS

For antique or designer furniture, auctions are probably the best venue for selling, the items can be viewed by prospective buyers in the auction house and they are taken away after the sale. Online auctions are good for high-value furniture, however, shipping costs to international territories may make selling in this way prohibitive. Smaller, more easily-shipped household items sell well at online auction if they are valuable.

Furniture dealers are best avoided unless you need to clear the items as quickly as possible, as they tend to pay lower prices for items. Classified advertisements are good for advertising furniture, particularly if you want to sell to a consumer rather than a dealer. The possible exception to this are the sale-on-consignment shops, which have an interest in getting the best possible price for the item, and pass most of it on to you.

PROPERTY

Property is one area where you may be better off by opting to sell via the traditional route of listing your property with an estate agent. For maximum exposure, consider going with more than one, although check that each allows properties to be registered with more than one and will not charge commission on the sale even if it is one of the other agencies that actually finds the buyer.

Estate agents usually take 2% of the selling price as commission, plus VAT. If you don't want to pay that, you can sell your property privately.

To set a fair price for the property, if you are selling privately, contact estate agents for a free valuation, try two or three and take an average on the prices they suggest. Put up a 'For Sale By Owner' sign and take out advertisements. Newspaper ads often attract would-be buyers. Place your ads in local papers, this will generally cost around 26p a word, so you target house-hunters in your area and try using a region-wide paper too, *Loot* is a good option. *Loot* offers a 12-week

property-selling ad package, costing from around £60 – depending on where you live. This provides you with an advertisement in the paper and a 'For Sale' sign to erect outside the house.

Another option is to use a property broker. These specialise in matching buyers with sellers. They charge a fee for advertising the property, but no commission. Many are internet-based like HomeWeb (www.HomeWeb.com), which has various advertising options ranging from around £50 to approximately £300.

While not paying estate agent fees is very attractive, DIY house-selling takes a lot of effort and time and you may well miss buyers who only look for property via agents.

Auctions are another avenue to explore, as sellers opt for both online and real-time means of disposing of property. Generally, however, this will not obtain you the highest possible returns and is usually reserved for properties that owners need to dispose of quickly. You can place a reserve price on your property, however, and property auctions are on a no-sale, no-fee basis. However, if a buyer is found, then you will pay commission to the auctioneers of between 1.75 and 2.5%, so although auctioning may be quicker, it will be no cheaper than using an estate agent. You will also have to pay for your property to appear in the auction catalogue and this will cost £200 upwards. On the plus side, buyers must pay 10% of the selling price straight away and completion of the sale must be agreed within 28 days.

FUTURE COLLECTIBLES

A s you will know by now, bargains come in many shapes and forms. They may be items you buy because you need them, but pay at below the market rate. Or they may be products you acquire simply because they are cheap. Then, there are those things you buy to sell on at a profit.

Having looked at the goods you may buy to sell relatively quickly at a profit, what about planning for the longer-term, as in ten or 20 maybe 40 years down the line? Just as items from a few years ago have become today's collectibles, which are those around today which will skyrocket in value in the future?

The knack is to be able to identify them ahead of time, so that you can buy now at retail prices and put them into storage for the time when they are worth much more.

WHAT MAKES A COLLECTIBLE?

A collectible is an item which is desired by one or more prospective purchaser. The reasons why people collect particular objects vary as widely as does the items themselves. Some hunt for goods associated with a famous person or fictional character. Others seek out those items which evoke their childhood, or another era, while many look for things associated with a profession, a country, a sport or a lifestyle.

Collectibles can be cheap or expensive, mass-produced or hand-made, ancient or modern. And don't let age fool you: even the most ancient item may be totally valueless if it is not desired by enough people, while objects dating from just a few years, months or even weeks ago can raise huge sums.

The key to a valuable collectible is rarity. An item increases in value in proportion to its popularity and in inverse proportion to its supply. If it is sought by many, but there are more who want the object than there are in circulation, then the laws of commerce dictate that the item will

FUTURE COLLECTIBLES

go to he or she who is willing to pay the most for it, hence the value rises.

Technically, however, extreme rarity can also work against value. If very few people know of an item's existence, then there may well be only a few who are interested in it.

This is one of the reasons for auction reserve prices. If an item is so rare that just one person is interested in acquiring it, then there will be no-one for them to bid against, and bidding will not rise. Hence, a reserve price will guard against an item going for less than its rarity commands.

This is why rarity – because an item was produced in very limited quantities or through the damage, destruction or loss – is the driving force behind the entire collector market.

To identify items that will increase in value, there are a few rules to observe:

1 Monitor trends

Desirability is influenced by fashion. When a particular look or style comes back into fashion, or there are a large number of people with an interest in a particular era and the items which evoke it, there is a knock-on effect on value. In particular, this affects areas such as the toy market. As new generations come of an age where they have disposable income, the value of good-quality items from their childhood era rises. When predicting future trends,

look at the most popular items among children and young adults today. In particular, note what items are disposable, are easily damaged

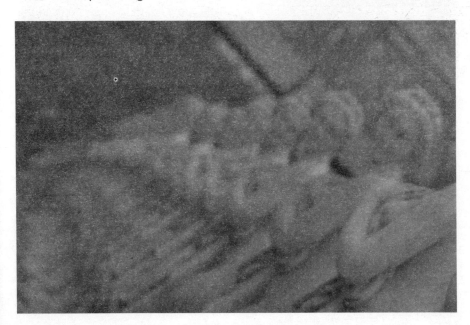

and replaced and will be superseded by new versions. These should be bought and stored for the future.

2 Condition

The highest prices are commanded by items in mint condition. Therefore, when you store goods for future resale ensure they are well kept: bubble-wrap and pack away carefully, making sure that the product's original packaging remains in as good condition as possible.

3 Don't hang on too long – prices can go down as well as up

Know when the market for a particular collectible is at its height; just as trends rise, so they fall. Price decreases are usually caused by a downturn in interest in the particular item or a glut of it on the market. For

example, the price of 1950s toys has decreased slightly of late, since many collectors of these toys are now ageing. As such, they move to smaller retirement properties and sell off their collections, putting more items in the marketplace and sating some of the demand in the process. As such, it is important to monitor the market for whatever items you have and know when to sell.

4 Beware of 'over popular' limited editions and 'collector market' products

With the rise of collecting as a hobby there are now innumerable products targeting the collectors' market, from model cars and ceramic plates to dolls and teddy bears. If you are searching for pieces which will increase in value, it may be wise to look elsewhere.

Collector-market products will almost always all be kept in good condition and when there is an infinite number of them, then however exquisite they are to look at, the value will almost never rise. The exception would appear to be limited edition runs.

But always check – if there are 50,000 items in this 'limited edition' then the rarity factor is zero. For the highest value increase, you should also aim for the lower end of this spectrum and eschew anything with a run of more than 5,000.

prove that it is genuine. When buying a brand, always go for the real thing, though don't completely discount cheap copies. These are often less well-made than the original and as such, fewer will last in good condition. A mint example will therefore be worth money to collectors of the original, even as a curio.

5 Authenticity

Always strive to prove the authenticity of an item, especially if it is linked to a celebrity. A certificate of authenticity for an autograph is a must if buying from a dealer. If the item is signed in person, try to obtain a photograph of this occurring to

6 Be mindful of product fragility

These days, goods are made from many synthetic materials unlike, say, toys produced during the 1940s which were mainly produced using poor quality metal because of the war effort. Many have corroded, making good condition pieces rare today. But

now items are cheaper to produce, they are also more disposable. This can be a positive factor for those collecting to sell in the future; the initial outlay is not only low but there will be relatively few items left in good condition by the time you come to sell. When storing, remember that plastic is extremely breakable and fades and biodegrades under certain conditions.

WHAT WILL BE COLLECTIBLE?

Gone are the days when only the most obvious items were collected – china, glass, stamps and postcards. As we have become flooded with consumer goods and durables so the spectrum of collectibles has widened.

Experts believe the following categories have collector growth potential:

1 Mobile phones

The leaps and bounds in communications technology renders models of mobile phones almost obsolete within a matter of months. Certainly, today's hottest models are light years away from the bulky, clumsy phones produced at the dawn of the mobile phone era in the late 1980s. In fact, with built-in cameras, email capabilities and MP3 players, they are even removed from phones produced just a few years ago.

As such, fans of communication are starting to show great interest in mobile telephony as an area of collecting, not least because mint, boxed phones are hard to find. To make sure your mobile will be valuable, make sure that all accessories are preserved along with the original box, packaging, leaflets, instruction manuals and software.

2 Computers and gaming systems

It wasn't so long ago that a home computer was a novelty, a humble machine with a monochrome screen and one-hundredth of the power of the cheapest models today. Similarly, the Sony Playstation 2 has superseded the PS1, which superseded a long line of machines going back to the likes of the Amiga and BBC micros.

Vintage computers, games and gaming systems are already big sellers with young collectors, eager to recapture the hours of childhood spent playing Pac Man and Tetris. In fact, there is a thriving market in replicas of these original games made to run on more modern machines. Again, these are items which swiftly became obsolete as they were superseded by newer, more powerful models and, as such, were often put into storage until they were eventually thrown out. When buying for investment, it is important to keep all packaging and ensure that the item stays free from any damage. A

wide selection of the most popular games, also kept in pristine condition, will boost the value, as it is likely that where now you need to find a working Nintendo to play *Pac Man* or similar, one day a PS2 will be a vintage item needed in working condition to play your rare, unscratched copy of the original *Tomb Raider.*

3 Designer items
Almost anything with a label has the potential for becoming collectable. But designer items should be chosen with particular care for investment purposes. Always go for one whose items best capture the ethos of the period. For example, original Mary Quant, Biba and Pucci designs from the 1960s sell very well. And don't just go for clothes. Seek out items with a designer name on them that are more likely to be disposed of, perfume bottles, for example, are a massive collector growth market, as are handbags and furniture.

4 Entertainment & sport
These can be big value-gainers as long as they are linked to the most famous names and products. Lobby cards or film posters for unsuccessful films will never be worth nearly as

much as those for smash-hit franchises, or for movies starring or directed by names who will be around for a long time. With all such items obtain as much proof of authenticity as possible. Look out for disposable goods – those things which would usually be thrown out such as posters, publicity material and merchandising. For example, in 1994, a newspaper offered James Bond-themed scratchcard games free inside its Sunday edition to coincide with the release of *GoldenEye*. While the prizes themselves would obviously have been great to win, similar fortune could be bestowed upon those who never scratched off the scratchcards, as unmarked ones are now very rare.

5 Toys

These are very popular collectibles. This is because they are the most likely items to be damaged or destroyed. Children's play is far more destructive than adults' every-day usage and this will lead to far fewer items surviving in pristine condition.

Firstly, go for popular brand-name items. If in doubt about what these are, check the annual lists of biggest-selling Christmas toys. These will be the ones tomorrow's adults will remember best and which they will want to seek out and own again.

Secondly, remember that playing with the toys is absolutely forbidden. If possible, buy two; one for play and one for putting away and keeping in immaculate condition. Even the most minor wear and tear reduces value. Go for toys that are tie-ins to popular TV series or films. This will greatly enhance desirability when it comes to putting them up for sale in the future. And look for products which have multiple pieces. The more components the toy has, the less likely it is that examples will survive with all the pieces intact.

6 Trendy items of cultural significance

Take a look around and note down trends and fads, however cheap the faddy item may be, especially if it is disposable or fragile. In the 1980s, Swatch watches were the height of fashion, but were also cheap and cheerful to appeal to fairly limited teenage budgets. These low-priced watches are now valuable collectors' items. So keep you eyes open; appraise anything you see in terms of its lack of durability, purpose, originality and relevance to the period. Chances are that if it stands out in any of these categories, it is a pretty good bet that somewhere down the line, someone will be willing to pay good money for it.

FUTURE COLLECTIBLES

USEFUL WEB LINKS

AUCTIONS & ANTIQUES

www.ukauctionlist.com – guide to property auctions in the UK

www.auctionpropertyforsale.co.uk – guide to property auctions in the UK

www.auctionhammer.co.uk - Guide to UK auctioneers (with information about antiques markets as well)

www.nava.com – National Association of Valuers and Auctioneers, an excellent resource for finding auction houses

www.british-car-auctions.co.uk – Directory of UK Car Auctions

www.autoseek.co.uk/car-auctions.htm - Directory of UK Car Auctions

www.disposalservices.agency.mod.uk – Government auctions

www.governmentauctionsuk.com – Government auctions listings

www.theantiquesdirectory.co.uk - Excellent resource for information about antique shops, markets and all things collectable

www.interantiques.co.uk – Another excellent resource for all things related to antiques

CAR BOOT SALES

www.carbootcalendar.com – Online listings of car boot sales across the UK

www.carbootjunction.com- Online listings of car boot sales in the UK

MARKETS

www.discover-paris.info/shopping.htm - Information on Parisian flea markets

www.fleamarketguide.com - Guide to US flea markets/swap meets

www.farmersmarkets.net - Guide to British food markets, with many useful links

www.allinlondon.co.uk/directory/13 26.php - Excellent listing of street markets in London

ONLINE AUCTIONS

www.eBay.co.uk – British eBay, the nation's premiere online auction site

www.eBid.co.uk – British online auction site

CLASSIFIED ADS

www.loot.co.uk – Online version of the popular advertising paper.
www.exchangeandmart.co.uk – Online version of the popular ad magazine
www.autotrader.co.uk – Online version of the popular classifieds paper dedicated to cars and vehicles
www.charityshops.org.uk – The Association of Charity Shops – excellent resource for finding information and branch locations

ONLINE CLOTHING OUTLETS & SECOND HAND SHOPS

www.ribbonsandpearls.co.uk – Online dress agency
www.allinlondon.co.uk/directory/119 1.php - Directory of London designer dress agencies
www.milliemoos.com – Children's online designer clothing outlet
www.Swerve.co.uk – Online designer clothing outlet
www.designer.co.uk - Directory of online designer clothing outlets
www.topoftheshops.co.uk/Clothing_a nd_designers - Directory of online designer outlets
www.dress-for-less.com – Online designer clothing outlet

SHOPPING WAREHOUSES

www.costco.co.uk – Shopping Warehouse company

CARS & LICENCING

www.hmce.gov.uk – Homepage of UK customs & excise department
www.dvla.gov.uk – Driver and Vehicle Licensing Agency

PROPERTY

www.propertybroker.co.uk – Information about UK property brokers
www.propertypad.co.uk – Information about UK propertybrokers
www.sequencehome.co.uk – UK estate agents
www.HomeWeb.co.uk – UK property broker
www.yourmove.co.uk – UK property resources
www.rightmove.co.uk – UK property resources
www.fish4homes.co.uk – UK property resources

TRAVEL

www.expedia.co.uk – Discount airline tickets, hotel bookings, etc
www.travelocity.co.uk – Discount airline and other travel tickets

SOFTWARE

www.download.com – Site with freeware software available for download

SEARCH ENGINES

www.google.co.uk – Popular search engine
www.yahoo.co.uk – Popular search engine

USEFUL WEB LINKS

A TO Z

Antique: Definitions vary, but the generally accepted rule is that an antique item is one that is not new, and usually more than 100 years old.

Auction: A sale whereby items are offered at a public gathering and sold to the individual who offers the highest amount during a bid. Auctions are increasingly held online.

Auction Paddle: A small sign given to bidders at some auctions. Raising this indicates making a bid.

Auctionee /Auction House: Organisers of auctions.

Bid: The amount offered by an auction attendee in attempt to purchase items on offer.

Certificate of Authenticity (COA): Applied to an item authenticated by a publicly known body or person such as a celebrity of historical figure.

Classifieds: Advertisements placed in publications by individuals wishing to sell items.

Collectible: Item which is desired by one or more people, less for its usefulness and more for its desirability, usually in companionship with similar pieces.

Collector-market product: Item produced specifically to be collected.

Commission: Amount taken from a final sales price by an agent executing a sale on behalf of a third party, in return for selling it.

Comparison shopping agent: An internet search engine allowing consumers to find similar products offered for sale on different websites and comparing the prices and specifications of these.

Dutch auction: When several identical items are offered at the same time, with more than one successful bidder.

Feedback rating: An eBay system by which users rate others on how satisfied they are with a particular sale.

Flea market: An area with many stalls selling diverse items, usually old and often in poor condition.

Increment: Amount by which an auction bid must be increased in order to out the previous bidder.

Limited edition: Any item where the production is halted after a certain amount have been produced.

Listing: Act of placing an item for sale on an internet auction site.

Lot: Item, or group of items, offered for sale at auction.

Loyalty scheme: Whereby a retail establishment rewards regular customers, usually via a redeemable points system.

Mint (condition): Descriptive term applied to an item in perfect condition.

Open outcry bidding: A form of bidding at an auction whereby the bidder signals openly to the auctioneer that they wish to place a bid on an item

Outlet store: A shop specialising in selling unused items which may have defects or are subject to conditions which prevent them being offered for sale through regular retailers.

Part exchange: Provision of an item in part payment for another, usually in a deal for less money than the original asking price.

PayPal: Online payment system used by individuals to accept and send money via the internet using credit cards, primarily to pay for online auction wins.

Pirate copies: Unauthorised software, films, music or any other recorded entertainment.

Reserve price: Tag placed on an auction item at the lowest amount for which the item will sell.

Rummaging: Act of searching through items for those which may be hidden or less visible.

Sealed Bid Auction: A form of auction, whereby bidders submit their bids in sealed envelopes, so that the others are unaware of what they have bid.

Second-hand: Term applied to a product which has already had one or more previous owner.

Seconds: New, unused items with slight damage or imperfections.

Secure connection: Encrypted internet connection to protect information from being viewed by third parties.

Stock: Items held and offered for sale by a retail establishment.

Storage Fees: Money charged by establishments such as auctioneers for keeping an item which no longer belongs to them.

Swap meet: Term derived from the US for a public antiques market. In the UK, this is an event for

dealers in particular antique/collectable items gather.

Timeshare scheme: Arrangement whereby, for a one-off or continuing payment, a participant is entitled to the regular use of a property or other item for a pre-defined period of time.

Username Password: Name chosen by an individual as their identification for a particular website, and a secret word allowing them to gain access to their account.

Vintage: Definitions vary, but the generally accepted rule is the term vintage is applied to items which are old, but not old enough to be officially classified as antiques, ie, less than 100 years.

Warehouse shopping club: Also known as a discount warehouse, this is a giant shopping venue, open only to members, where food and other items are sold in bulk at low prices

Wholesale: Term applied to items sold in great bulk at lower per-item cost than if were sold individually.

JARGON BUSTER